JOHN STICKL

FOLLOW THE CLOUD

HEARING GOD'S VOICE
ONE NEXT STEP AT A TIME

MULTNOMAH

FOLLOW THE CLOUD

Trade Paperback ISBN 978-1-60142-925-4
eBook ISBN 978-1-60142-926-1

Published in the United States by Multnomah, an imprint of the Crown Publishing Group, a division of Penguin Random House LLC, New York.

MULTNOMAH® and its mountain colophon are registered trademarks of Penguin Random House LLC.

Library of Congress Cataloging-in-Publication Data
Names: Stickl, John, author.
Title: Follow the cloud : hearing God's voice one next step at a time / John Stickl.
Description: First Edition. | Colorado Springs, Colorado : Multnomah, 2017.
Identifiers: LCCN 2017014027| ISBN 9781601429254 (pbk.) | ISBN 9781601429261 (electronic)
Subjects: LCSH: Providence and government of God—Christianity. | Listening—Religious aspects—Christianity. | Spirituality—Christianity.
Classification: LCC BT135 .S825 2017 | DDC 248.4—dc23
LC record available at https://lccn.loc.gov/2017014027

Printed in the United States of America
2017—First Edition

10 9 8 7 6 5 4 3 2 1

SPECIAL SALES

Most Multnomah books are available at special quantity discounts when purchased in bulk by corporations, organizations, and special-interest groups. Custom imprinting or excerpting can also be done to fit special needs. For information, please e-mail specialmarketscms@penguinrandomhouse.com or call 1-800-603-7051.

"In a time where 'how to' manuals abound, it is a refreshing book you hold in your hands. John Stickl, as a young and successful megachurch pastor, chooses to engage us not with selling a model but rather inviting us to a timeless principle of hearing God's voice and taking next steps with boldness. I've been privileged to see him and the Valley Creek Church family practice what they preach. Framed within the conviction of God's acceptance, godly community, and God's purpose for your life, you will be deeply inspired! Read it and live it!"

—ALAN PLATT, leader, Doxa Deo and City Changers
Movement, global

"If you are a follower of Jesus, your journey with him is an adventure about taking next steps. John hits the mark in *Follow the Cloud* with encouraging God's sons and daughters to continue to advance his kingdom by feeling secure in their identity, relationship, and purpose in his son, Jesus. I highly recommend this book for anyone who wants the confidence that they can hear God's voice so they have the faith to take their next step."

—CHAD HENNINGS, three-time Super Bowl champion,
author of *Forces of Character* and *Rules of Engagement*

"Pastor John is one of the brightest young leaders in the American church, and I am grateful he has written this book! His voice is much needed right now, and I believe your faith will be strengthened and increased as you turn each page."

—BRADY BOYD, senior pastor, New Life Church,
Colorado Springs, and author of *Addicted to Busy*

"I love John Stickl's heart and mind for leadership. His approach is fresh, nuanced, and challenging. Regardless of the size of church you lead, John is a thought-leader for next generation ministry."

—CAREY NIEUWHOF, author and founding pastor,
Connexus Church

"God desires to have an intimate relationship with us, and it's his voice that draws us closer to the very heart of God. In *Follow the Cloud,* my friend John Stickl explains how hearing the still small voice of God and obeying his call will lead us into a deeper, more passionate relationship with him."

—ROBERT MORRIS, founding senior pastor, Gateway Church, Dallas/Fort Worth, and best-selling author of *The Blessed Life, The God I Never Knew, Truly Free,* and *Frequency*

"A playbook to life's greatest lessons filled my mind while reading *Follow the Cloud.* If we want to experience all that God has to offer, then we must be still and trust that 'The Good Shepherd leads you through the valley you don't want to go through to get you to green pastures you need.' This book is a must-read for all mighty men and women of God. I thank God for the power, courage, faith, strength, love, and guidance of the life that is John Stickl. He literally breathes life into others through his words."

—DONALD DRIVER, Super Bowl champion and *New York Times* best-selling author

"John Stickl reminds us that so much of being a leader, and so much of following Jesus, is taking the next step. One foot in front of the other. Pushing forward. Discovering and stepping into the new and unknown. And true influence is as much about following as leading. *Follow the Cloud* will encourage and inspire you on the journey!"

—BRAD LOMENICK, founder of BLINC, author of *H3 Leadership* and *The Catalyst Leader,* BradLomenick.com, @bradlomenick

"John Stickl's writing in *Follow the Cloud* is clean and clear, kind-hearted and thought-provoking. *Follow the Cloud* is valuable for everyone who places too much weight on what they do over who they are, which means most everybody needs to read this book."

—RICK BEZET, lead pastor, New Life Church of Arkansas, and author of *Real Love in an Angry World*

FOLLOW
THE
CLOUD

*To Colleen, there is no one else I would
rather go on this adventure with. Oh,
the places we will go . . . together.*

———

*To Trey and Emma Joy, may you
always have the courage to follow
the cloud because God is good,
Jesus has forgiven you, you are
loved, and everything is possible.*

CONTENTS

INTRODUCTION

I t *is* about you.

I realize those are not typical words you would expect from a pastor. I mean, when was the last time you heard a sermon series called "It's All About You"? You probably never have and never will. Those four words make us feel uncomfortable. Honestly, they make me feel uncomfortable. We have been told our entire lives that it's not about us. We have heard countless messages telling us to always put others first. We have been taught that God *needs* us to do great things for him. And although we have been full of good intentions, maybe we have unintentionally placed unhealthy expectations upon each other. You know the kind: *Try harder. Do better. Change your behavior. Bury your feelings. Fix yourself. It's not about you anyway, so pull yourself together.* And from experience, I can tell you that is an exhausting way to live.

But what if it *is* about us? What if it is more about us than we have realized? What if our lives are more about what God wants to do *in us* than what he wants to do *through us*? What if the journey that God invites us on is really about discovering who we are, who he is, and what we were created to do?

Maybe God is more interested in setting us free than making us religious.

To be honest, I am afraid to write this book. I know that's not a very inspiring way to start, but it's true. My life is full. I am leading a large, fast-growing church. My kids are young and full of energy, which means I am constantly tired. I have very little free time. And I am not sure how to take what is in my heart and put it on paper. But here's the thing: I think this is my next step. I believe that God is inviting me to do this. The very act of writing it is what the heart of this book is all about. *Following the cloud—courageously taking next steps when we see God move.* I am following the cloud because in many ways writing this book is about me. It's about following God to a place I have never been before to discover things I have never seen before. And that is the invitation I believe God is extending to you—to follow the cloud. To go places, do things, discover truths, and find a freedom you have never experienced before.

I mean, let's be realistic: it's not as if God really needs us to accomplish his purposes. I don't know about you, but I have quickly realized that I don't have all that much to offer anyway. God didn't need Noah to build the ark. He didn't need David to kill Goliath. He didn't need the disciples to establish his kingdom. And he doesn't need us to change the world. In fact, if you don't feel very qualified, you are in good company. Yet for some reason, he always chooses us. This sometimes mysterious God has chosen broken, hurting, and confused people to follow him to places they have never been before. Why? Because it is his deepest desire to set us free. "It is for freedom that Christ has set us free" (Galatians 5:1). He longs to break off the limits, labels, and insecurities that fill our hearts and minds. Every next step he asks us to take is an invitation to live in the freedom of his love, a discovery that without him we will never make. God is a loving Father who wants his children to live beyond the brokenness of this world—the brokenness many of us never seem to get free from.

You see, God knows something we tend to forget: the greatest thing we can do for others is become the healthiest versions of ourselves. I can't love my neighbor if I don't love myself. And the reality is, very few of us have a *healthy* love for self. "We love because he first loved us" (1 John 4:19). John, the Apostle of Love, reminds us that we can't give what we have yet to receive. And people in bondage can't lead others to freedom. So if you want to live a life that is not about you, you first have to embrace that following him *is* about you.

But not in the way you think.

It's about you awakening to life. It's about you discovering who God says you are. It's about you and finding freedom from your past. It's about you resting in his love. It's about you receiving the fullness of the finished work of Jesus. It's about you submitting to his

> The greatest thing we can do for others is become the healthiest versions of ourselves.

Lordship. God is most glorified when your heart is alive and free, and you can become that person only by following the cloud.

So what is the cloud? Well it's a physical picture of a spiritual truth hidden in the ancient story of the Exodus. "By day the LORD went ahead of them in a pillar of cloud to guide them on their way and by night in a pillar of fire to give them light, so that they could travel by day or night" (Exodus 13:21). Can you imagine what that would have looked like? The entire nation of Israel following a pillar of cloud during the day and a pillar of fire by night. The presence of God leading them from slavery to the Promised Land. Of all the ways God could have led his people, he chose to do it through a personal and ever-present cloud. Because that is who God is: intimately personal and always present. This cloud represented his tangible presence. It defined their identity, surrounded them with his love, and led them into a land of freedom. From within this mighty cloud, he spoke with the gentleness of a whisper: *Follow me, one next step at a time. When I move, you move. When I stop, you stop. Where I go, you go. Keep your eyes on me. Stay in step with the cloud, and I will lead you to discover who you are, who I am, and what you were created to do.*

Following the cloud is how I have learned to live my life and how our leadership team leads our church: listening to God's voice and following his presence by faith wherever he goes. And although I don't always understand what he is doing, I have learned that every time I have the courage to follow, I learn more about who I am, who he is, and what I am created to do. Every time I follow, he awakens more of my heart. With every next step, I see a little bit more of Jesus and become a little bit freer of myself. And that is the same journey I believe he is inviting *you* to take.

A JOURNEY OF THE HEART

When we read about the Israelites following the cloud from Egypt to the Promised Land, we tend to focus on the physical aspects of their journey: like wandering in the desert, gathering manna from heaven, and fighting the nations of giants. But what we often fail to realize is that the Exodus was really a journey of the heart. While God was leading the Israelites out of Egypt, through the wilderness, and into new lands, he was actually leading their hearts out of bondage, through their fears, and into new lives of wholeness. The goal wasn't just to get them to a new land; it was to help them learn to live free as beloved children of God. Every physical next step was an invitation toward emotional, relational, and spiritual freedom. The physical journey of the Exodus was the process, but freedom of the heart was the outcome. The same is true for us today. While God is leading us through what often feels like our own Exodus, the goal isn't to find the perfect life; it's to heal and free our hearts. A journey of next steps isn't really about where we go, what we do, or what we accomplish; it's about who we become.

At the church where I serve as a pastor, Valley Creek Church, we have a simple illustration that captures this truth, which we call the three circles—or *life in the Father's heart*. We believe that as we receive his grace, we are drawn to experience his presence and then are empowered to release his kingdom—that as we discover our new identity in Jesus, it will lead us into relationship with him and empower us to live out our purpose. At the center of where these three circles intersect is the Father's heart for us. Jesus said, "I am the way and the truth and the life. No one comes to the Father except through me" (John 14:6). Jesus is the way, but the Father is the destination. Jesus came not only to show us but also to lead us into the love of the Father. The Father's heart is the Promised Land, and it's where the cloud is always drawing us

one next step at a time. This is the pattern you find all throughout
Scripture.

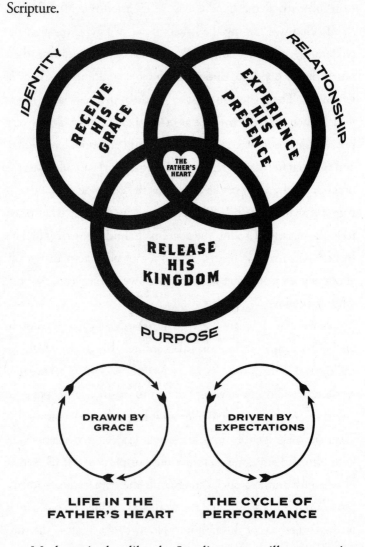

My hope is that like the Israelites, you will start moving
toward the freedom of living in the Father's heart one next step at
a time. And our movement always starts with receiving his grace.

When we receive his grace, we will experience his presence and release his kingdom. As we receive our new identity, we will run to relationship with him and live out our purpose. When we believe we are beloved sons and daughters, we will desire to be with our Father and will spend our lives building his kingdom. When we know we are forgiven, we will joyfully approach him and live with courage. But the inverse is also true. If we resist his grace, out of fear we will avoid his presence and will strive to earn his approval. If we believe we are spiritual orphans, we will be afraid of the Father and will spend our lives building our own kingdoms, trying to find significance. If we don't know who we are, we won't know how to relate to him and won't know what we were created to do.

> We believe that as we receive his grace, we are drawn to experience his presence and then are empowered to release his kingdom.

Sounds simple enough, right?

We are drawn by grace, not driven by expectations. But unfortunately this world is full of expectations. So instead of *life in the Father's heart,* we are often driven through *the cycle of performance* (the three circles in reverse). Starting with circle 3, we spend our lives performing, trying to earn God's approval so that we can become significant. We strive to behave to gain God's acceptance so that we might earn our forgiveness. In *the cycle of performance,* we go against the current of grace: we *do* in order to *become.* And as I already said, that is an exhausting way to live.

Order is everything.

Identity leads to relationship, and relationship releases purpose. This is where the cloud led the Israelites and where it is leading us. This *is* the gospel. The gospel isn't just for salvation; it is for all of life. And it is always drawing us to live free as beloved sons and daughters. If at any point in this book you get stuck, refer back to these three circles and remind yourself that the grace of Jesus is leading you into the freedom of the Father's heart: the ultimate Promised Land.

Restful Movement

All throughout the Bible, clouds are pictures of promise, presence, protection, and prophetic potential. That is a great description of a Spirit-led life. The first time the word *cloud* is mentioned is when God gave Noah a "rainbow in the clouds" (Genesis 9:13) as a promise of his goodness. "The Lord came down in the cloud" to be with his people (Numbers 11:25). "He spread out a cloud as a covering" (Psalm 105:39) to protect his people in the world. And, finally, Jesus said the nations of the earth "will see the Son of Man coming on the clouds of the sky, with power and great glory" (Matthew 24:30). The cloud is always revealing the Father's heart to his beloved sons and daughters. We are following the cloud toward him, and he is riding the cloud toward us.

Following the cloud is simply a life of restful movement. We rest *in* Jesus and yet never stop moving forward *with* him. Like the first-century Christians, we are the "followers of the Way" (Acts 9:2, NLT). We have nothing to achieve, prove, or earn. We have everything to receive, discover, and explore. We restfully move in step with him. That is the *way* of Jesus.

So here is my question and challenge for you: What if you had the courage to follow the cloud—to listen to God's voice and respond to his presence, to move when he moves and stop when he stops? You might not fully understand it, and it might not always make sense, but you can trust that he is always leading you toward your Promised Land. In fact, your next step is often in the direction of your greatest fear. He leads you toward your fears so that you can become fearless in his love!

The cloud is moving in your life right now, leading you toward his freedom one next step at a time. Maybe he is inviting you to follow him into a new job, a new career, a new relationship, or a new school. Maybe he is inviting you to let go of something old or pick up something new. Maybe he is inviting you to extend forgiveness, release generosity, share your story, or give up your addiction. Maybe he is inviting you to break out of the rut and routine you've been stuck in for years. I don't know what your next step is, but I know he wants you to get to your Promised Land even more than you do.

And your Promised Land isn't a destination; it's a revelation of who you are, who he is, and what you were created to do. It's life in the Father's heart. And although you may not even be aware of it, he is there. Calling. Drawing. Inviting you to follow. Inviting you home.

One.

Next step.

At a time.

AWAKEN TO LIFE

THE FATHER WANTS YOU TO BE FREE

A CLOUD APPEARS

By day the LORD went ahead of them in a
pillar of cloud to guide them on their way and
by night in a pillar of fire to give them light,
so that they could travel by day or night.

—Exodus 13:21

W e want to offer you the job!"

Those were the words I longed to hear. Finally, a little
bit of hope appeared in the midst of my pain—or so I thought. I
had just come out of an incredibly hard season. For more than six
months, it felt as though my world was falling apart. I had recently graduated from college. I was full of dreams. I knew where
I wanted to go, what I wanted to do, and what my life was going
to be like. I had great plans. And naively, I thought the world
would embrace those plans. That is, until my life was swept away
by the crashing waves of brokenness.

In six short months, my life was completely flipped upside

down. My heart was broken by an unexpected breakup. I watched a woman crash her car and held her in my arms as she took her last breath. I was in a crazy accident that totaled two brand-new Jet Skis and put my best friend in the hospital. While working on a construction site, I was shot with a nail gun. I probably should admit that I was the one who accidentally pulled the trigger. Talk about embarrassing. I ended up in the emergency room so many times that they knew me by name. I was caught in a riptide of chaos and couldn't figure out which way was up. Full of anger, frustration, and pain, I wondered where God was.

So when the call came from the police department offering me a job, I was filled with hope because I finally saw a way out. It had always been my dream to become a police officer. And not just a police officer, but a SWAT team member or FBI agent. I wanted a job full of action and adrenaline. I had trained, studied, and prepared, and finally all *my* hard work was going to pay off. My dream could begin and I could move on with my life. But as soon as I hung up the phone, I had an experience that I'd never had before. I heard this small voice inside me whisper, *You know this isn't what I have for you.* "Wait, what was that? I must have had some seriously bad pizza last night. That was weird."

But again I heard, *You know this isn't what I have for you.* I had no idea what was happening.

And then a third time, *You know this isn't what I have for you. The door is open and you can take it if you want, but I have so much more for you.* I thought, "You have got to be kidding me! For the first time in my life I'm hearing God's voice and he is taking away my dream. Doesn't he realize how much pain I have just experienced? Doesn't he understand how desperate I am for a new beginning? Doesn't he know this is what I have been working toward?" His words just kept echoing in my heart: *This isn't what I have for you.*

Have you ever had a moment like that? When you felt like God was completely interrupting your life? When your longing to hear him speak was quickly replaced by your desire for him to be quiet?

So I asked out loud, "Then what do you have for me?" And you know what I heard? Nothing. Absolutely nothing. The sound of crickets.

It is always interesting how silent God can be when we ask him about the details of our future. Rarely does he give us the full picture. More often than not, he gives us one simple next step. A step that often makes no sense. A step that feels like it's in the wrong direction. To say it another way, God speaks in sentences not paragraphs because you can only obey one sentence at a time. And although it may be frustrating that he doesn't give us all the details, it's actually his love at work. God knows that if he gave us all the details, we would be so overwhelmed that we wouldn't follow. If we knew everything he had in store for us, the whole story, we would turn and run in the opposite direction. "No eye has seen, no ear has heard, and no mind has imagined what God has prepared for those who love him" (1 Corinthians 2:9, NLT). God's invitations are always bigger than our imaginations. And this invitation was way beyond my imagination.

I am convinced that if he would have shared with me all the details of my future that day, I would have said no. Actually I would have said, "No way!" But he didn't. He simply invited me to trust him just enough to take one small step. And so after days of wrestling, and against all reason, I called the department back and declined the offer. I hung up the phone and said out loud, "Okay, God, now what?" And so began my journey of following the cloud.

THE BEGINNING OF FREEDOM

I don't know if you have ever noticed this, but the Old Testament can often seem completely irrelevant to our lives. I mean, what does killing giants, sacrificing animals, or following a cloud have to do with us today? There are some really random passages in the pages of our Bibles. But although those ancient verses may seem unimportant, they offer us more than we often realize. The Old Testament is full of physical pictures that reveal spiritual truths—stories that give us deep spiritual insight into the reality of our lives. A great example of this is the story of the Israelites.

The physical story of the Israelites is in many ways our spiritual story. Although that is not the most flattering comparison, it is probably an accurate one. A people enslaved by the world, stuck in a way of life they have no hope of escaping, confused about who they are and disillusioned about the hidden God of their forefathers. Most of us know what that feels like. To feel unnoticed and insignificant. To be hopeless and afraid. Wondering where God is. Thinking we have been forgotten.

Yet God never forgets. He always remembers and he always moves. After four hundred years of the Israelites being slaves in Egypt, God said, "I have indeed seen the misery of my people. . . .

I have heard them crying out . . . and I am concerned about their suffering" (Exodus 3:7).

And so he moved, because the heart of God is drawn to the cries of man.

God remembered his people and did the unexpected. He raised up a deliverer named Moses and set them free. Through some of the most profound miracles in all of history, God had a showdown with Pharaoh. The most powerful man on the face of the earth and his empire were defeated in a matter of a few days through the ten plagues. This is a great reminder that "if God is for us, who can be against us?" (Romans 8:31). Even the most powerful enemy is no match for God. And just like that, more than a million slaves were turned loose into the desert.

Now, just stop and think about that for a minute. What do you do after four hundred years of slavery? Where do you go? How do you live without someone telling you what to do every minute of every day? What many of us see as the pinnacle moment of the Israelites' lives was actually a terrifying event. We often forget that is how salvation feels for many people today. They are afraid of the very freedom that Jesus offers.

As soon as the Israelites were released, they were faced with a choice. It's the same choice I was faced with the day I heard God speak.

Option one for them was to go back to slavery—back to a life they knew, a life that in many ways was *comfortable*. Hear me out here, okay? Being a slave was predictable. They had homes, food, and jobs. Life was *safe* within the rhythm of their routine. In

Egypt, they knew how to live. Not only had slavery become a comfortable way of life, it had become their identity. Unfortunately, that often describes the typical American life. We have become so defined by the bondage of our dead-end jobs, bills we can't pay, miserable routines, the shame of our past, and relationships that are falling apart that we actually find comfort in our brokenness. We feel safe when we know what to expect, even if what we expect is the full force of a taskmaster's whip. Sometimes we prefer the security of slavery to the unknown of freedom.

Option two was to follow God—a God they were still unsure about, a God who was inviting them to step into the unknown by faith. All they knew was that this God had promised to take them to a land flowing with milk and honey: a Promised Land. It was a choice that wasn't as easy as we might think. Could they really follow a God they didn't know? Could they trust him to take them to a place they had never been before? Were they willing to give up whatever control they had left? It's a choice many of us struggle with today.

> Sometimes we prefer the security of slavery to the unknown of freedom.

Reluctantly, they chose to follow because the gravitational pull of God's grace was stronger than the resistance of their fear.

By Cloud, By Fire

But how do you lead more than a million people into a new way of life? How do you mobilize a sea of humanity to start moving toward their destiny? You give them a cloud and lead them one next step at a time. "By day the LORD went ahead of them in a pillar of cloud to guide them on their way and by night in a pillar of fire to give them light, so that they could travel by day or night. Neither the pillar of cloud by day nor the pillar of fire by night left its place in front of the people" (Exodus 13:21–22).

From the moment the Israelites stepped foot out of Egypt, God invited them to follow the cloud. God knew they would need his supernatural grace to move forward, so he provided a cloud for them to follow. The cloud was his tangible presence. By day it was a pillar of cloud, by night a pillar of fire. God provided exactly what they needed: a promise, his presence, and a next step. He gave them a living cloud so that in every moment of their journey, they could simply lift their eyes and see his presence. He wasn't just *in* the cloud; he *was* the cloud.

By day, the cloud covered, protected, and surrounded them in a harsh desert. By night, it brought them warmth, light, and comfort in the midst of the darkness. When the cloud moved, they moved. When the cloud stopped, they stopped. Where the cloud went and how it moved didn't always make sense. Sometimes it seemed to move too quickly. Other times, not fast enough. Sometimes it would go the long way around and then take a sudden shortcut that seemed dangerous. But even though they didn't understand this cloud, it was their life. It was the love of God on display. And it was going to lead them to discover who they were, who he was, and what they were created to do. It was a journey that was going to be about them. One that would expose, reveal, heal, and restore.

Remember, God wasn't just leading them *out of* Egypt; he was leading them *into* the Promised Land. He wasn't just leading them *out of their* slavery; he was leading them *into his* freedom. And he led them with his presence. He led them with his love. Following the cloud was a risk, but not following the cloud was an even greater risk.

Courageously taking next steps when God moves—following the cloud—is a physical picture of a spiritual truth. It's a revelation of what this journey with Jesus is all about. When we have the courage to follow his presence and respond to his voice, he leads us *out of our* bondage and *into his* freedom one next step at a time. And remember, God never leads you *out of* something without leading you *into* something better.

The Israelites followed an actual cloud, the disciples followed Jesus on earth, and today we follow the Holy Spirit. The Old Testament cloud is a picture of the Spirit-led life. "Since we are living by the Spirit, let us follow the Spirit's leading in every part of our lives" (Galatians 5:25, NLT). Today the cloud

> God never leads you *out of* something without leading you *into* something better.

isn't above us; it's within us. The Spirit of the living God is leading us toward Jesus's promise of abundant life (see John 10:10). We aren't always sure where it is going. We don't always understand it. But we can be confident that he is leading us to life. And like the Israelites, all we really need is a promise, his presence, and a next step.

Unexpected Invitation

After I declined the job offer, it was, let's just say, a *really* long week. I must have asked God a hundred times what was next. I prayed. I read the Bible. I journaled. I listened. I asked people if I was going crazy. Some of them told me I was. I was looking for anything. But as in any relationship, you can't make God speak. All I knew was he had something else for me. But what was it?

Finally, after days of waiting, I heard his voice again: *I want you to be a pastor.* "Dear Lord, you have got to be kidding me! That is the worst idea I have ever heard. You have the wrong guy. I don't know how to be a pastor. I just heard your voice for the first time last week. I don't like church. I don't even go to church. I don't want to be a pastor. Christians are boring, and they always look miserable. I'm going to call back the police department and take that job."

I want you to be a pastor. Ugh! It was my next step and I knew it. It was an unexpected invitation—an invitation I never wanted. I wonder if that is how Peter felt when the cloud first appeared in his life?

Peter had to have been blindsided by Jesus's invitation to be a disciple. He was a no-name fisherman with a simple plan to build a fishing business, raise a family, and live a quiet life. It's not as though Peter had a great résumé. He is most often remembered for his failures. Peter wasn't on anybody's draft board. He was just living his life and doing his thing. But that all changed when the cloud started to move.

I sometimes wonder what that first day would have been like for Peter. His life was full of nights of failed fishing. Day after day. Week after week. Month after month. Year after year. Trying to fill his boat with fish. Trying to make a living and build a life for his family. But no matter how hard he tried, he never seemed to get ahead. The Gospels paint a picture of a guy who didn't really know how to catch any fish, which is really bad news if you are a fisherman. His big dream of being a successful fisherman was far from becoming a reality. And what he did have was far from inspiring.

I think we can resonate with Peter's story. We spend our lives working hard, but we never seem to catch anything. We strive. We perform. We achieve. We try to build things our way. We try to find significance. We chase a dream that we ourselves aren't even inspired by. Sure, we may have acquired some possessions, accomplished some things, and won some awards. But we know we still haven't really caught anything. We haven't found what we are looking for because, honestly, we aren't even sure what we are looking for. But all of that was about to change for Peter. And it can change for you.

> At the heart of every next step God asks us to take is a revelation of more of Jesus.

One morning, after another night of failure, the cloud appeared in his life. Jesus came walking down the shore and said, "Come, follow me, . . . and I will make you fishers of men" (Matthew 4:19). *Follow me and I will make you. Peter, let go of your boat and I will make your life.* The cloud was on the move and promised to calm the storms that raged in Peter's heart if he would have the faith to follow.

This is a familiar verse, but in a lot of ways we have missed the depth of it. We often believe that Jesus was inviting Peter to follow and that he is inviting us to follow because *he needs us to do things for him*. We think we have to follow him so we can behave better, become more reli- gious, earn his approval, or maybe just so he won't be mad at us. You know, the whole "God

> We have to remember that Jesus isn't a recruiter; he is an inviter.

needs us to change so we can change the world" thinking. But the truth is that Jesus invites us to follow him for our good, not his. He invites us to follow so we can see him more clearly. At the heart of every next step God asks us to take is a revelation of more of Jesus. He *makes* our lives by showing us himself.

Following the cloud allows us to see who he really is. In Egypt, the Israelites knew about God, but only in following the cloud did they get to *see* God. On the shore, Peter had heard about Jesus, but only in walking away from his boat did he get to *see* Jesus. We have an idea of who Jesus is, but it's only in following that we actually get to *see* him. Every next step allows us to see a part of him we have never seen before. And the more clearly you see Jesus, the more clearly you see everything else.

What felt like an interruption that day was really an invita- tion. Life's interruptions are more like divine invitations. Jesus loves to get our attention by disrupting our routine so he can per- sonally hand us an invitation to live. We have to remember that

Jesus isn't a recruiter; he is an inviter. He isn't out there desperately recruiting us to be part of his army, sales team, cleanup crew, or church-nursery force. No. Instead, he is walking down the shore of our often-uninspiring, dreamless lives, inviting us to freedom. Inviting us to leave behind our way of life to come and see more of him. We follow. He makes. And his ability to make is always greater than our willingness to follow.

Jesus didn't call Peter because he needed Peter to do great things for him. Jesus called Peter because he wanted to do great things *for Peter.* He is always inviting the least-deserving, least-expecting people to come follow him. To leave it all behind and follow the cloud. *When I move, you move. When I stop, you stop. Where I go, you go. Follow me and I will make you. Together we will get there one next step at a time.* And so with an outstretched hand, Jesus removed Peter's fear with love and extended an unexpected invitation.

Jesus wasn't asking Peter to let go of his boat so he could take something away from him. He was asking him to let go of his boat so he could give everything to him. However, to be positioned to receive, one has to first be willing to let go. God can give to only those whose hands are open and ready to receive.

I certainly didn't understand what God was inviting me to when I first experienced the cloud moving. It felt as if he were asking me to do some ridiculous things that seemed crazy to everyone around me. But by his grace, I found the courage to follow—to say yes. One little next step after another ultimately led me to decline the police job, go to graduate school, serve as a pastoral intern, meet my wife, move to Texas, join a church-staff team, have kids, become a lead pastor, and write this book. With every next step I have taken, my heart has seen a little bit more of God. I have watched him do miracles I never would have dreamed of seeing. I have seen parts of his kingdom I never knew existed. One step changed the direction of my entire life. Proverbs 16:9 says, "In his heart a man plans his course, but the LORD determines his steps." I have learned that God's steps are always better than my plans.

I am convinced that if God would have showed me that night all he'd had in store for me, I would have taken the police job. There is no way this kid from Buffalo, NY, could have handled the thought of moving to Texas, let alone being a pastor! But God didn't show me his whole plan. He just shined his light on the next step.

Jesus is the narrow gate that leads to a wide life. Following him doesn't constrict our lives; it actually expands them. I now believe that Jesus wasn't asking me to let go of my dream so he could take something away from me. He was asking me to let go so he could give everything to me. He was inviting me to receive. He was inviting me to be free.

The same is true for you. He has seen your misery, he has heard your cry, and he is concerned about your suffering. And so he has come. Jesus comes to you with an invitation to take a simple next step out of the old and into the new. He doesn't want you to do great things for him; he wants to do great things for you. He isn't trying to take anything away from you; he is trying to give everything to you. He is inviting your feet and your heart to leave the shore behind.

Come, follow me and I will make you!

"Where are we going?" *You'll see.*

"How long will it take to get there?" *Awhile.*

"Will it be easy?" *No, but I will be with you.*

"What will it be like when we get there?" *Better than you can even imagine!*

Follow the Cloud—Live Free

Consider viewing life's interruptions as divine invitations. What is currently interrupting your life? And what do you think God might be inviting you to do?

If pressed to say what step God is asking you to take right now toward freedom, what would you say? It may be a huge, risky step, or it might be something incredibly simple.

2

COME AND SEE

They call it the happiest place on earth, and we couldn't wait to go. For six months, my wife, Colleen, and I had been planning to surprise our kids with a trip to Disneyland. Emma was four and Trey was six, the perfect ages for the Magic Kingdom. They were still young enough to want autographs from the characters. They were finally tall enough to ride most of the rides. And they had the childlike hearts to believe that every princess was real. But how do you explain the grandeur of Disney to little kids who have never experienced it? I am not sure you can, so we decided to surprise them. All we told them was that in a few weeks, we were going to go "somewhere special."

The day we were supposed to leave for the airport, we were caught off guard, as neither of our kids wanted to go. In fact, they refused to go. They were having so much fun in the pool that they didn't want to get on a plane to go "somewhere special." "Dad, we just want to swim." Regardless of how hard we tried, we couldn't convince them that where we were going was better than the pool. Cue the temper tantrums. "We don't want to goooooooooooo." I remember thinking, *Do you know how much this is costing me? Get out of the pool!* Finally, so we wouldn't miss our flight, I said, "Let's go, because we are going to Disneyland." Within ten seconds, both of them were out of the pool and waiting in the car.

That wasn't one of our family's best moments, but it gave me a great picture of a profound truth: Wherever God is leading you is always better than where you have been. The future with God is always better than the past without him. If God is love, then everything he asks you to do is loving. Every step he invites you to take is a step designed for your good and his glory. Remember, in the kingdom we always go from glory to glory and from victory to victory. If it seems like he is taking something away, it's because he wants to give you something better. The Promised Land was better than Egypt. The palace was better than the pasture. The upper room was better than the shore of Galilee. But it always takes faith to follow when we aren't really sure where we are going.

Following the cloud doesn't mean your circumstances will always be better; sometimes they seem to get worse. It doesn't mean everything will be easier; it often feels harder.

> Wherever God is leading you is always better than where you have been.

It doesn't mean that there won't be challenges; there will be. But everywhere he leads you is always better than where you have been, because he is there. Following the cloud isn't about having perfect circumstances; it's about living in the presence of his perfect love—a love that frees us from self, fear, and the worries of tomorrow. When the cloud moves in your life, don't throw a temper tantrum and miss your flight. Disneyland is always better than the pool. Always. But you have to get out of the pool!

Vision Isn't Cheap

Have you ever noticed how challenging it can be to describe profound things in simple words? For example, how do you tell someone what Niagara Falls is like? How can you paint a picture of the Grand Canyon in conversation? How do you explain what it's like to hold a new baby who is only minutes old? There are some things in life that are so beyond our vocabularies that the only thing we can do is just invite others *to come and see.*

Following the cloud is similar. It was impossible for God to describe to the Israelites what the journey would be like because they didn't have the ability to comprehend the great things he had in store for them. So he simply invited them to come and see.

If we're honest, this is the part of following Jesus that we usually resist the most. And why we often don't get out of the pool. I don't know about you, but I don't want to come and see. I want to see and then decide if I want to come. Show me what it is going to be like, tell me how I am going to feel, give me all the details of how it will work, and then I will decide whether or not I am interested. As a matter of fact, I'd love to see the ending before we get started. I'd prefer a spoiler alert, thank you very much.

But God has a better way. He invites us to follow by faith,

being sure of what we hope for and certain of what we do not see (Hebrews 11:1). Faith is the certainty that we will see good things with each step we take. It's the belief that every step is taking us "somewhere special." And when our hearts have the faith to come, we will have the eyes to see. A heart full of faith gives us eyes full of vision. It's the willingness to come that creates the ability to see.

Think of the disciples. Jesus invited twelve men to leave the familiarity of their lives to come and see the superior reality of the kingdom of God. He didn't give them any details. He just said, "Come . . . and you will see" (John 1:39). And so by faith, "they went and saw" (verse 39). With each next step, they saw lame men walk, lepers cured, blind eyes opened, demons cast out, miraculous provision released, and dead people raised to life. It was their willingness to come that initiated their ability to see. They had to risk stepping away from their boats before they saw heaven come to earth.

The same is true for us. If we want to see Jesus as a healer, we have to follow him into the lives of sick people. If we want to see him as a peacemaker, we have to follow him into a storm. If we want to see him as a miracle worker, we have to follow him into desperate and hopeless situations. It's in the moments we tend to avoid where Jesus is most clearly seen. Jesus leads us into the places we would never choose to go so he can show us things we would never be able to see.

But what if the disciples would have said no? What if they would have refused to step into the unknown because they didn't have all the details? Think of all they would have missed. Peter wouldn't have walked on water. The disciples wouldn't have seen Lazarus raised back to life. They wouldn't have experienced the outpouring of the Holy Spirit. They would have still been sitting in a fishing boat, holding an empty net. Which is where a lot of us still are: sitting in our boats, holding empty nets because we are afraid to follow. We are waiting for Jesus to show us all the details before we are ready to move. And because he doesn't usually give us the details, we don't come, so we are unable to see. Many of us have been unable to see the abundant life because we have been unwilling to come. So maybe a lack of miracles in our lives has less to do with God's desire to move and more to do with our reluctance to follow.

Missing Out

The first time I heard the term *FOMO,* I thought someone was cursing at me. FO what? Apparently, I'm not very hip.

FOMO, aka fear of missing out, is a driving force of our culture today. There is a fear of missing out on parties, events, games, activities, pictures, and so on. Many people go to great lengths to avoid missing out on the things of the world.

And while most of us have at least a little bit of worldly FOMO, what if we lived with heavenly FOMO? What if we started to make our decisions with a filter of not wanting to miss out on the great and mighty things that we do not yet know (see Jeremiah 33:3)? What if every time we saw God move, we responded because we didn't want to miss what he was doing? What if we were more concerned about missing out on kingdom moments with Jesus than missing out on group selfie pics, stock options, or tenure? That is the heart of a cloud follower.

A few years ago, God invited me to take a simple next step. He asked me to go first and reconcile with someone I had no interest in reconciling with. I know that sounds awful to admit. Every week I try to inspire people to reconcile with Jesus and the people in their lives, but in this instance, I just couldn't bring myself to actually go first. So I started negotiating with God. Maybe you know how this goes: *God, I can't right now. I'm busy. I'll do it next week.* Graciously, God waits a week and then asks you again. *God, I know I should, but I have to prioritize my family time right now. I know you want me to focus on my family. I'll get around to it later.* A few weeks go by, and again he gently asks you. *I am going to do it, I promise. Tomorrow. I'll call him tomorrow.*

Tomorrow comes and goes. Again he asks, but now you start to get annoyed at his patient persistence. *God, he was the one who was wrong anyway. He should apologize to me. As soon as he calls me, I'll forgive him.* A few weeks later, you hear the sacred echo again. It's as if no matter where you go or what you do, you can't get away from this step. It is amazing how unrelenting God can be. That's what following the cloud is like. Once you are aware of it, you can't pretend it's not there.

For a few months, I just kept negotiating with God. My heart refused to follow, and I kept justifying why I couldn't take this step. Then one day I woke up to discover that I had received a text message from this person congratulating me on our church's new campus, along with an apology for his part of the issues of the past. As I read and reread his text, humbled by his message, I realized I missed my chance to go first in reconciling a relationship that was broken over some very small things. He went first and did what God had asked me to do.

As tears filled my eyes, I felt the gentle voice of the Lord again. *Johnny, the reason I wanted you to go first and reconcile with him was because I was going to show you more of myself in that moment. I wanted you to take that step so you could see more of me. I want you to follow me so you can be free.*

That was a defining moment in my walk with God. That day, I realized he wasn't trying to make my life harder; he was trying to reveal something to me. But I wasn't willing to come, so I wasn't able to see. I missed out. I knew God wasn't mad at me, but I was heartbroken that I missed experiencing more of him. I never want to experience that feeling again. I don't want to be a *God negotiator;* I want to be a *cloud follower.*

AHA MOMENTS

I would bet that just like my story, there have been countless times where God has asked you to do something that you didn't understand. Our lives are full of moments when nothing about what he was asking us to do seemed like a good idea. When his invitation came, it challenged every bit of logic we had. Moving to a new state. Quitting that job without first securing a new one. Giving generously to someone else when feeling as if we don't have enough for ourselves. You'll find situations like this throughout the Bible. God has a habit of inviting us to walk on water.

For example, there was a guy named Naaman. He was told to go wash in the river seven times to be cured of leprosy. *Um, no thanks. Since when does water cure leprosy?* Or do you remember when Jesus told the disciples to feed five thousand people with two fish and five loaves of bread? *Really, Jesus? That isn't even enough to feed twelve kids, let alone twelve men.* Or how about when the Israelites were told to march around the city of Jericho for seven days and on the last day blow a trumpet

> We don't understand and then obey; we obey and then we understand.

and the walls would fall down? If I were an officer in that army, I would have said, *Joshua, you're crazy! We're out of here.* The Bible is full of moments in which people didn't understand but did obey. When we read the accounts of those stories, we discover that understanding always comes through obedience. As they obeyed, the aha moment appeared.

This is what it's like to follow the cloud. We don't understand and then obey; we obey and then we understand. I want you to read that again: we obey and then we understand. Obedience always precedes understanding. In fact, obedience is the key that unlocks the mystery of what we don't understand. Hebrews 11:3 says, "By faith we understand." We have to choose to release our need to logically understand what can only be discovered by faith. It is a spirit of faith that leads to a mind that understands. Aha moments come only to those who follow by faith.

When the cloud moves, it often doesn't make sense to us or anyone else in our lives. What do you think Peter's mother-in-law thought about him quitting his fishing business to follow a no-name rabbi? What did Noah's kids think about their dad building an ark in the desert? What did Sarah think when Abraham said, "We are going somewhere but I have no idea where"? None of them knew what to expect. They just saw the cloud moving, so they followed. The aha moment wasn't found in the invitation; it was found in the obedience.

Over the years, I have watched countless people obey when they didn't understand. And although their circumstances have been different, they all had one thing in common: They were focused on Jesus. Their eyes were locked on the Author and Perfecter of their faith as they followed him out onto the water. Their paths were made straight (see Proverbs 3:5–6). They had peace even though they didn't understand (see Philippians 4:7). They found the elusive joy many of us are still looking for (see Romans 14:17). And for some reason, when they were walking on the water, they didn't really care about why he asked them to do it because they were too busy enjoying him. They were too busy *walking on water!*

When God invites us to follow, he doesn't answer all our questions. Actually, he often creates more questions than we already had. We will never fully understand what God is inviting us to because it is too big for him to describe. He just says, "Come and see." This is the great adventure of a faith-filled life.

CONNECT THE DOTS

I remember going out to eat with my family as a kid and loving it when the restaurant would have a kids' menu with games on it. I am sure my parents did too. It's amazing what a few crayons and some games can do for kids. One of my favorites was the one where you would connect the dots to create a picture. Do you remember those? The page would be full of dots in random places with numbers attached to each of them. All you had to do was start at 1 and draw a line to 2, then 3, then 4, and so on. What initially seemed like a random smattering of dots would ultimately create an amazing picture. The hidden picture would emerge only after all the dots were connected.

That is how I believe God invites us to live our lives: unsure of the final picture but with the courage to take simple steps in the order he gives them to us. And the goal isn't just to finish the picture but rather to enjoy the journey.

Usually God will show you only your next step and the direction you are going. "Your word is a lamp to my feet and a light for my path" (Psalm 119:105). He is a lamp that shines on your next step and a light that points in the direction you are headed. That is all he will show you because he wants you to be desperate for and dependent upon him, the Light of the World. Withholding all the details forces us to focus on him instead of trusting in ourselves.

Jesus knows that if he told us all the details of the future, we wouldn't be able to handle it. "There is so much more I want to tell you, but you can't bear it now. When the Spirit of truth comes, he will guide you into all truth. He will not speak on his own but will tell you what he has heard. He will tell you about the future" (John 16:12–13, NLT). Jesus tells us that we aren't ready for everything he wants to share with us, so he has given us the Holy Spirit. He promises that the Holy Spirit will tell us what we need to know exactly when we need to know it. Our job is to simply take the step in front of us—to, by faith, live to the full extent of the revelation we have. All we have to do is connect the dots, and the best possible picture of our lives will emerge.

God says, *Step here.* We respond, *But I thought we were going that way.*

God says, *Step here.* We respond, *But that doesn't make sense.*

God says, *Step here.* We respond, *But I don't like this step.*

God says, *Step here.* By faith, we respond, *Okay, Lord. Because you say so, I will follow.*

Every one of us has to decide how we will live our lives. Are we going to build our careers based on the best wisdom of the day? Are we going to pursue our own personal happiness? Are we going to lead our families the way everyone else leads theirs? Are we going to build our churches based on the latest church-growth strategy? Or are we going to follow the cloud? Proverbs 16:25 says, "There is a way that seems right to a man, but in the end it leads to death." Paraphrased, what initially looks good to us is often the worst option. I am tired of taking the path that looks good to me but turns out to be a dead end. I have learned that God's path is often the opposite of what I would choose on my own. In fact, to follow him means doing a whole lot of things that don't seem to make sense. If God's ways are higher than our ways, then his steps for us will rarely align with the wisdom of this world, but they will always align with the wisdom of heaven. God will ask us to give when we want to take, forgive when we want an apology, serve when we want to be served, stay when we want to go, and go when we want to stay. Heavenly wisdom doesn't always make sense in earthly circumstances, but it will always lead you to life. When we follow Jesus's *way*, we will discover his *truth* and experience his *life*. (See John 14:6.)

Following the cloud is the key to a regret-free life.

A friend of mine recently resigned from his executive-level, high six-figure-income job because he believes that was what God was inviting him to do. Walking away from the American dream is most people's nightmare, but not for him. His heart is full of peace, and his life is full of joy. He has no idea what is next. He has no other job lined up. He just knows that he heard the whisper of the Lord inviting him to follow the cloud—to take this next step. He believes that where he is going is better than where he has been and that God is leading him "somewhere special." His heart of faith is giving him eyes to see.

I want to have that kind of faith.

1—2—3—4—You don't have to have it all figured out—just—connect—the—dots. God leads us in small steps, not giant leaps. What is the next dot he is inviting you to connect? An amazing picture is emerging.

Come and you will see!

Follow the Cloud—Live Free

Understanding the aha moments of life comes through obedience. Recall your most recent aha moment. What did you come to understand about God? About yourself?

God leads us in small steps (dots), not giant leaps. Think back over the last six months, looking for any "dots." Now look to see how they might be connected. If your view is hazy, ask God for clarity in connecting the dots.

3

MOMENTUM

Here is a confession. I love change. But I only love it when it's my idea or when I am telling someone else how he or she should change. Just ask my wife or my team. I am really good at telling other people that they need to take a next step. But when it comes to change in my own life, I resist it.

For most of us, change is a four-letter word. We are annoyed when our favorite restaurant changes its menu. We are frustrated when the cable company changes our channels. We get irritated when technology changes faster than we can keep up. For instance, how come every time I buy a phone, they come out with a new one that makes mine obsolete? And why do I have to upgrade my operating system? I like it just how it is. Let's not even talk about how much we despise change in church. We don't like change.

The more established we become in life, the more we resist change. There is something about predictability that offers us a perceived sense of security. We feel safe with that which we can expect. We feel safe with that which we can control. And change forces us into the unknown.

Let's just say it how it is. Change is uncomfortable.

But to follow the cloud is to change. If we are ever going to move forward, we have to have the courage to choose change over comfort. And although it isn't always comfortable, the short-term pain of change leads to the long-term transformation we desire.

One-Wing Butterflies

Inherent in this journey with God is the understanding that we will continually embrace change. To walk with Jesus is to change. The gospel is not just a message of good news; it's a message of change. We come to him as we are, but he refuses to allow us to stay as we are—which is great news for the people in our lives.

I like to say it like this: *God will never allow you to always remain the same.* His relentless love refuses to allow you to settle. He will apply whatever pressure necessary to keep you in a continual process of transformation. We follow the unchanging God of change. Although he never changes, everything he invites us to involves change. "If anyone is in Christ, he is a new creation; the old has gone, the new has come!" (2 Corinthians 5:17). Like a caterpillar, in Jesus we experience a metamorphosis. When a caterpillar is changed into a butterfly, there is such a complete transformation that what *was* can no longer be seen in what *is*. No one would ever confuse a caterpillar with a butterfly.

> God will never allow you to always remain the same.

But did you ever wonder what that process feels like for the caterpillar? I am not sure it's the most pleasant experience. After filling up on nature's salad bar, you settle in upside down for a nice long nap. As you wrap yourself in your favorite silk-blankie cocoon, you doze off into deep sleep while listening to the sound of serenading crickets. Life is good. But then suddenly you wake to tummy rumbles and strange sensations. Unsure of what is happening or how to stop it, you patiently wait, hoping it's a bad dream. Then out of nowhere, giant wings start popping out of your back, long legs start popping out of your side, and antennas start popping out of your face. Surprise!

Now I don't know about you, but I'd much rather fly as a butterfly than crawl as a caterpillar, even if it requires the awkwardness of embracing change. We were never meant to crawl around in the mud; we were meant to soar in the sky. In Jesus, the old is gone, and the new has come. What *was* can no longer be seen in what *is*. Your new life with Jesus isn't confused with your old life without him.

But sometimes we get stuck. Sometimes, because of the discomfort, we quit changing before we have grown both wings. And a one-wing butterfly will never fly.

MOVING ON

Sadly, the Israelites almost never got off the ground. After God defeated Pharaoh, they were finally set free. The tenth and final plague, the Passover, was their moment of salvation. Victory was declared. Pharaoh let God's children go. But as the Israelites began to follow the cloud out of Egypt, Pharaoh decided he wanted the people back. Pharaoh (the king of darkness) always wants the people back, so he chased after them with soldiers, horses, and chariots. And although he had already been defeated, he used the only weapon he had left—intimidation.

It's a good reminder that whenever the enemy is defeated, the only thing he has left to do is intimidate us. He will growl in our lives trying to evoke fear in our hearts, trying to convince us that we have been or will be defeated, trying to make us surrender and return to our bondage. But don't forget, your enemy has already been defeated. He only has the authority to bark, not bite. So keep moving.

But that's easier said than done. Because sometimes there are obstacles that make it seem like it is impossible to continue on the journey. The cloud is moving, but the way through isn't always clear to us.

Even the Israelites found themselves in what appeared to be a dead end. In front of them was the Red Sea, a gigantic body of water that seemed impossible to cross. Behind them was the angry Egyptian army, chasing them with a spirit of intimidation. On one side there was the sound of thundering horses and shouting soldiers, and on the other the sound of crashing waves. They were stuck—stuck in the space in between. They were no longer slaves, but they weren't yet living in freedom. They had been saved from death, but they had yet to step into life. They had been brought out of Egypt, but they hadn't yet entered into the Promised Land. They were stuck in between the past and God's promise, and they had three options: they could give up and go back to slavery; they could stand their ground and fight the Egyptians, a battle God had already won; or they could have the faith to follow God out of their comfort zone across the overwhelming Red Sea.

Like it was for the Israelites, it's easy for us to get stuck in the space in between. God has rescued us from the kingdom of darkness. Through Jesus, we have been set free from our slavery, taskmaster, and Pharaoh: sin, shame, and Satan. "He has rescued us from the dominion of darkness and brought us into the kingdom of the Son he loves" (Colossians 1:13). Victory is ours. We start following the cloud, but just like that—*wham!*—we can find ourselves stuck. We have the faith to follow God out of the old, but we don't have the faith to follow him into the new. We have met Jesus, but we haven't discovered the abundant life. We are no longer caterpillars, but we haven't yet become butterflies. It's as if we live somewhere in between the cross (the forgiveness of our sins) and the empty tomb (the resurrection life). And it's a miserable place to be. I have been there, and I bet you have too.

The space in-between is a desperate place—a dry desert. It's a place where we are not satisfied and live with a sense of discontentment. Where life is defined by routine and going through the motions. Where we rev our engines and spin our wheels but make no progress. We can't go back to where we came from, and we haven't yet gotten to where we are going. Life isn't what it was, but it certainly isn't what it's supposed to be. We're stuck. And for many of us, this becomes home. It becomes our new norm. We start to believe this is as good as it gets. We start to believe God doesn't fulfill his promises. But it's not that he hasn't fulfilled his promises; it's that we haven't had the faith to follow. All of God's promises belong to us, but we have to have the faith to claim them. So we settle down in places God wanted us to simply pass through. We stop taking next steps, and we choose to settle where we were never meant to live. We resign to the lives of one-winged butterflies.

> The Israelites weren't stuck because the cloud wasn't moving; they were stuck because they weren't following.

I love what God says to Moses, what he says to us when we get stuck: "Why are you crying out to me? *Tell the Israelites to move on.* Raise your staff and stretch out your hand over the sea to divide the water so that the Israelites can go through the sea on dry ground" (Exodus 14:15–16). The Israelites weren't stuck because the cloud wasn't moving; they were stuck because they weren't following. The cloud was leading them through the Red Sea, but they wanted to go back to Egypt. They followed the cloud, only to question it when the change became uncomfortable. So God said, *Hey, let's stop complaining, let's stop looking back, and let's not settle here. You have been here long enough. It's time to move on. Take a next step. I will part these waters. Follow me through what seems impossible, because my promises are waiting on the other side.* The only way to get unstuck is to take a step into what seems impossible. And like a loving father calling his young child to jump into the pool, God gently says, *I promise I will catch you.*

It's important to remember that we never get stuck in life because God isn't moving; we get stuck because we stop following. Like the Israelites, we always have three options. We can go back to living in bondage—back to the brokenness and pain of the past. We can spend our lives fighting the battles God has already won—fighting the shame, addictions, regrets, abuse, relationships, and failures that have already been defeated. Struggling in an endless battle with an enemy that has already been rendered powerless. Or we can follow by faith and cross over into the unknown of change.

The choice is yours. But until you choose to cross over, the horses and chariots, the worries and cares of life, will never stop chasing you. God's love allows them to pursue you until you become desperate enough to follow him where you would never choose to go on your own. And while we may hate it, desperation is actually God's grace because it can take you where you didn't have the faith to go.

NEW VOCABULARY

I don't know if you've ever noticed this, but God has a tendency to lead us into seemingly impossible situations. He loves to lead us to the shore of our own Red Sea to see if we will have the faith to follow. God wants us to confront the impossibilities of life so he can show us his limitless power. He leads us to the things we are afraid of so he can make us fearless in his love. In other words, God likes to erase the always and nevers in our hearts.

So here's a suggestion. What if together we agreed to ban those two words from our vocabulary? What if we stopped using *always* and *never* in our daily lives? *Things will always be this way. This will never get better. I will always have to do this. I will never be free.* I wonder how often we declare those two words over our lives or how often we whisper them to ourselves. We have created a self-imposed prison, trapped by the bars of *always* and *never*. We have convinced ourselves that so many things are impossible. But the only *always* and *never* that are true is that God will always be with you and that he will never leave you or forsake you (see Matthew 28:20; Hebrews 13:5). Nothing is impossible with God.

So what is your Red Sea? What's that thing that seems impossible to cross? Where are the words *always* and *never* causing you to pull back from where God is leading? Maybe it's quitting that job where you have seniority in order to start a new career. Maybe it's moving away from where you have spent your whole life to a place you have never been. Maybe it's forgiving that person who broke something

> The only *always* and *never* that are true is that God will always be with you and that he will never leave you or forsake you.

deep inside of you. Maybe it's adopting a child. I don't know what yours is, but many of us have turned our backs toward the crashing waves and are stuck fighting battles God has already won. Remember, your future is always on the other side of your fear. You might be just one step away from breakthrough. You might be just one step away from a totally different life. It's time to erase *always* and *never,* because with him everything is possible.

Out of the Box

Unfortunately, many of us don't believe everything is possible because we have put God in a box. Let me explain.

I love Christmas, but I hate Christmas decorations. Okay, that's a strong statement. It's not that I *hate* decorations; it's that I highly dislike putting them away. No matter how hard I try, I never can fit them all back in the box. The giant six-foot tree never fits back into the original twelve-inch box. Our ornaments, wreaths, snowmen, and nativities don't fit in the one rubber tote we have. Eight miles of tangled lights can't fit into the carryout box from Costco. Christmas decorations are amazing when they are on display, but they never were meant to fit in a box. So every year, I find myself trying to jam a store's worth of decorations into a few small boxes. And I quickly lose whatever Christmas spirit I have left.

We have that same problem with God. We try to force him into a box that is way too small. We want him to fit into a space we can control—a box with a cover and handles that is safe to carry and store in the attic. But to put God in a box is to place our own limitations upon him. And whenever we limit God, we instantly get stuck.

For many of us, our past experiences have shaped our theology. We have allowed our experiences to determine what we believe instead of allowing what we believe to create what we experience. Put another way, our experiences have formed the size and shape of the box we put God in. Many of us believe God can't. God won't. God isn't. Because somewhere along the way, our experience taught us that God couldn't. God didn't. God wasn't. So we question his power, willingness, and goodness. We create a box, a framework of limitations, that we try to stuff him in. But when we place limitations around God, we unintentionally place limitations around ourselves. I can't. I won't. I'm not. And when we place limitations around ourselves, we also place limitations around others. They can't. They won't. They aren't. It's a vicious cycle that leads to defeated lives.

But God is bigger than your box. He is more loving, forgiving, powerful, merciful, and compassionate than the box you keep him in. And the only way to expand the borders of your box is to follow him into the impossible—to cross your Red Sea. He leads you into the unknown because he wants you to see that he cannot be covered or carried. He invites you to explore the limitless expanse of himself one next step at a time. "I pray that you, being rooted and established in love, may have power . . . to grasp how wide and long and high and deep is the love of Christ" (Ephesians

3:17–18). In other words, *may God explode your box.* He won't ever fit into any box, because he is meant to be on display. Don't lower your theology down to your personal experiences; raise your experiences up to your theology.

He can. He will. He is. Which means . . . You can. You will. You are.

Do You Want to Get Well?

The pool of Bethesda was, shall we say, interesting. It was a gathering place for the broken—people who had put God in a box. Its sides were crowded with the damaged, sick, and disabled. Sores, disease, and filth clung to those who made their home there. The continual sound of painful moaning, heartbreaking cries, and hopeless prayers filled the air. These were desperate people. These were stuck people. No change. No life. No future. The last place we would choose to visit was one of Jesus's first stops in the book of John.

"Do you want to get well?" (John 5:6).

That is probably one of the most thought-provoking questions Jesus asked anyone in the Gospels. Just stop and think about this. Here is a paralyzed man who has been an invalid for thirty-eight years. Thirty-eight years! He has been unable to walk, care for himself, or pursue his dreams. His entire life is defined by a three-foot-by-six-foot mat. He is the ultimate example of someone who is stuck. His brokenness is his Red Sea. And Jesus asks him, "Do you want to get well?"

I can imagine the disciples thinking, *Come on, Jesus. Look at the poor guy. Of course he wants to get well. Of course he wants to walk. Just heal him and let's get out of this nasty place before we catch something.* But Jesus asks the man directly, "Do you want to get well?" Why? Because Jesus knows that if we don't want to get well, he can't force us to be.

Jesus can't make us receive the life that he offers.

A lot of us are really good at talking a big game. We talk about wanting to be healthy. We say we have a desire for breakthrough. We act as though we want to get unstuck and be free.

> The familiarity of shackles is often more comforting than the unknown of freedom.

But when it comes right down to it, when Jesus asks us, "Do you want to get well?," our answer is often no. We don't really want to get well, because we have found our identity in our brokenness. Our lives are defined by those jobs we hate, the toxic relationships we are in, the skepticism we have, the addictions we are gripped by, or the mundane routines we constantly complain about. As much as we like the thought of getting well, we don't know who we would be without our mats.

If we are honest, sometimes we prefer godless security to God-led change.

Our brokenness can easily become our comfort. The familiarity of shackles is often more comforting than the unknown of freedom. It certainly was for this man.

"'Sir,' the invalid replied, 'I have no one to help me into the pool when the water is stirred. While I am trying to get in, someone else goes down ahead of me'" (John 5:7). What an interesting response. The man gives Jesus a bunch of excuses for why he is the way he is and why he hasn't changed. But he doesn't answer the question Jesus is asking. Jesus isn't asking him why he is stuck; he is asking him if he wants to get well.

But it's all too easy to offer excuses for where we are in life. We can easily explain why we are stuck or why we can't change. We have been hurt, misled, taken advantage of; we haven't had the right opportunities; no one has helped us; and so on. You probably know the list as well as I do. And although all those things may be true, what if we stopped looking back at *what* and started looking ahead at *who*? This man was so busy focusing on his brokenness that he forgot to look at the Healer standing right in front of him. Jesus was inviting him to move from being a victim to being victorious.

The cloud was there to heal those who were willing to move on. But sometimes the first step is the hardest one. The law of inertia says that things at rest stay at rest and things in motion stay in motion. And while that is true in physics, it is also true in life.

Do you want to get well? Then "'Get up! Pick up your mat and walk.' At once the man was cured; he picked up his mat and walked" (John 5:8–9).

Spiritual momentum begins with a single next step.

There has always been something about this story that has bothered me. After Jesus healed this man, why didn't anyone else say, "Jesus, heal me too"? There were sick people all around the pool who just witnessed this healing, yet no one else cried out for help. Even though they were a single step away from a brand new life, they just watched Jesus come and go. If you were the sick person sitting right next to this guy, wouldn't you ask for healing too? Why didn't this one miracle ignite a healing revival? Maybe it was because no one else really wanted to get well, because to get well is to change. Maybe they were content spending their lives stuck in the comfort of their brokenness instead of following Jesus into the unknown of lives of wholeness.

Do you really want to get well? Then pick up your mat, take a next step, and walk.

It's Just Peanut Butter

A few years after 9/11, I went on a mission trip to Pakistan. Definitely not one of the wisest things I have ever done. I should have known it wasn't a good idea when we had to sign a form saying the government would not come rescue us if we got captured. For ten days we traveled all over the nation praying that the people would have an encounter with Jesus. It was incredibly intense, and I was incredibly glad to get home.

Toward the end of the trip, I started to get really sick. A crazy fever, the shakes, the chills, bathroom visits, bloodshot eyes, and foggy thinking all set in at the same time. You name the symptom, I had it. Somehow I had caught Dengue fever. What is Dengue fever? I didn't know either, but I pray you will never know *the Dengue Fever.*

As we were leaving the country, our team got to the airport

security check, and as they searched my bag, they found my treasured half-eaten jar of peanut butter. I'm a picky eater, and peanut butter was my main food source on the trip. Apparently, they had never seen peanut butter before and were highly concerned with this creamy substance. They took one look at me—a six-foot-one white guy from America with a giant beard, bloodshot eyes, and the shakes—and concluded I was a drug smuggler high on drugs.

As they "escorted" me to the detention area, I just kept thinking, *I want my mom.* All I could picture was spending the rest of my life rooming with some terrorist in a Pakistani prison.

After sitting in a small cell for what seemed like hours, two angry Pakistani officials came in and slammed my jar of peanut butter on the table. They kept asking me what it was, what I was on, and what I was smuggling. Seriously!

Finally, after doing my best to convince them it was only food and that I wasn't a smuggler, they agreed to let me go but only if I left the peanut butter behind. I gladly parted with the tasty jar that had kept me alive for the past ten days and boarded my flight, grateful to be going home.

It's amazing to think that the only thing that was keeping me from where I was going was a half-eaten jar of peanut butter. I would have been crazy to choose a jar of peanut butter over my freedom, yet we make that choice all the time. We hold on to the very things that hold us back.

The rich young ruler is a great example of this. When he asked Jesus how he could find life, "Jesus looked at him and loved him. 'One thing you lack,' he said. 'Go, sell everything you have and give to the poor, and you will have treasure in heaven. Then come, follow me.' At this the man's face fell. He went away sad, because he had great wealth" (Mark 10:21–22). The last thing this guy wanted to talk about was the first thing Jesus addressed. If I were the rich young ruler, I would have been thinking, *Really, Jesus? My money? I'll gladly join a small group, invite someone to church, serve my neighbor, or do anything besides give away my money.* But because love always meets the highest need of the other person, Jesus was willing to risk his walking away in order to set him free. Jesus pressed on the one thing that was holding him back. But because this man refused to let go of his money, he couldn't get to where he wanted to go. He held on to his peanut butter and missed his flight.

I wonder what you might be holding on to.

I wonder what might be holding you back. Maybe it's money, a job, a relationship, an offense, a hobby, an addiction, an ungodly belief, comfort, fear, anxiety, religion, or your past. The last thing you want to talk about is probably the first thing Jesus wants to address. If you're not sure, then have the courage to ask a few people in your life, "What do you think is holding me back from following Jesus?" Sometimes they have a more accurate perspective than you do.

> You have to let go of what is in your hand if you want to discover what is in his heart.

As important as you think that thing is, it's just peanut butter. It's not worth being stuck. Freedom is better than a jar of Jiffy. Whatever Jesus is offering you is better than what you have.

I know it's hard to let go of something that has brought you comfort and identity, but because Jesus loves you fiercely, you can hold on to the things of life loosely. You have to let go of what is in your hand if you want to discover what is in his heart. The cloud hasn't brought you this far to leave you stuck now.

Maybe it's time to put the peanut butter down.

Follow the Cloud—Live Free

Would you describe yourself as a person who embraces or resists change? What's a change you've gone through in the past year? If you embraced it, what have you learned? If you resisted it, how's that going?

How has your view of God been shaped by the words *always* and *never*? In what areas of your life have you unintentionally placed God into a box? Take a little time to ponder that last question; don't answer too quickly.

RECEIVE HIS GRACE

WHEN YOU KNOW WHO YOU ARE, YOU
DON'T WANT TO BE ANYONE ELSE

4

OVERWHELMING KINDNESS

> Because of your great compassion you did
> not abandon them in the desert. By day the
> pillar of cloud did not cease to guide them
> on their path, nor the pillar of fire by night
> to shine on the way they were to take.
>
> —Nehemiah 9:19

Recently, I was thinking about some of the times in my life when I just completely blew it—moments where I messed up and embarrassed myself. It was a much longer list than I care to admit.

I can still hear the sound of crunching plastic from when I totaled my dad's brand-new Jet Ski. I remember when I was busted for lighting my neighbor's pumpkins on fire one Halloween night. I'll never forget having my paper ripped up for cheating in calculus class. And my rear end is still sore from the time I wrote "Johnny was here" all over the walls with my mom's nail polish. Yeah, it's a long list.

But one of my favorite failures, if there is such a thing, was the first time I baptized someone. He was a giant of a man—at least six foot seven. A huge crowd had gathered around the tank and I was so nervous. My hands were shaking, my voice was trembling, my heart was pounding, and I just wanted to get it over with. So I said, "I baptize you in the name of the Father, and the Son, and ummmmm." My mind completely froze and I forgot the Holy Spirit. So I panicked. I quickly tried to get him under the water, but because he was so tall, I was able to dunk him only up to his neck. His head never went under. Awkwardly, he looked up at me, and neither of us knew what to do. I guess I could have shoved his face under with my hand, but that wouldn't have been good for anyone. So with no other options, I pulled him up. Everyone in the room burst out in laughter, and I wanted to disappear. I mean as the baptizer you have only one job: say the traditional line and get the guy all the way under. Somehow I managed to mess that up. Needless to say I wasn't invited to baptize anyone else for a long time.

To this day, the people who were there harass me. They jokingly ask, "Did that baptism even count? Because you never got him all the way under and you never said the words *Holy Spirit!*"

I bet your life has been full of messes just like mine. You probably have a list of your own that is all too easy to recall. Some of those failures you can laugh at now, while others may still be incredibly painful. Based on how other people have responded to our failures, we have become conditioned to be ashamed, hide, and even pay for our mistakes. Our past experiences have created our present expectations. We often expect the worst from others because we have experienced the worst, and unfortunately we apply those expectations to God. So instead of following the cloud, we often hide from it.

But maybe Jesus is different from our expectations.

GO FISH

One of my favorite examples of this is found in John 21. Let me set the stage of the story. Peter is a mess. I know, I know—what a surprise.

Just a few days earlier, Jesus told the disciples that he was headed to the cross and that they would all deny him. Peter, in the way that only he could, stepped forward and declared his allegiance to Jesus: "Even if I have to die with you, I will never disown you" (see Matthew 26:31–35). In that moment, Peter made the classic mistake we still struggle with today: he was more focused on his commitment to Jesus than on Jesus's commitment to him. Instead of saying, "I will never disown you," Peter should have been declaring, "You will never disown me." Life is not about what we do for Jesus; it's about what he has done for us. Cloud followers are more focused on God's faithfulness toward us than our faithfulness toward him, because even "if we are faithless, he will remain faithful" (2 Timothy 2:13).

Jesus replied, "Oh, Peter, I know you're trying, but before the rooster crows, you will deny me three times. But even after you fail, I will come and find you" (see Matthew 26:34). And that's what happened. Peter denied Jesus to a servant girl. The sound of failure rang out through the air as the rooster crowed, and Peter was broken. He tried hard and he fell even harder. Sometimes it seems as though the harder we try, the worse we fail. Peter was defeated and hopeless. Jesus was gone. So he ran to his favorite hiding place: the Sea of Galilee.

> "I'm going out to fish," Simon Peter told them, and they said, "We'll go with you." So they went out and got into the boat, but that night they caught nothing.
>
> Early in the morning, Jesus stood on the shore, but the disciples did not realize that it was Jesus.
>
> He called out to them, "Friends, haven't you any fish?"
>
> "No," they answered.
>
> He said, "Throw your net on the right side of the boat and you will find some." When they did, they were unable to haul the net in because of the large number of fish.
>
> Then the disciple whom Jesus loved said to Peter, "It is the Lord!" As soon as Simon Peter heard him say, "It is the Lord," he . . . jumped into the water. . . .
>
> Jesus said to them, "Come and have breakfast." . . .
>
> Jesus came, took the bread and gave it to them, and did the same with the fish. (John 21:3–7, 12, 13)

Peter blew it. And what do we do when we fail? We go to whatever brings us comfort. For Peter it was fishing. What is it for you? Maybe you find comfort in your job, a hobby, a relationship, a substance, Facebook, or Netflix. When we fail, we run to whatever we find comfort in. We run to whatever we can control. So Peter ran back to his boat.

But I don't think he was really focused on fishing that night. I think the reel of shame was playing over and over in his mind. I think that as he held an empty net in his hand, he kept rehearsing his mistakes to the echo of the rooster's crow. Shame is a cruel master that gets deep into our hearts through the door of failure. It makes us relive our worst moments at the worst times. It is unrelenting and leads us to find refuge in the things of this world, pursuing comfort in things that can only numb, not heal. Shame never sleeps.

But neither does Jesus.

So early in the morning, the resurrected Jesus showed up on the shore of Galilee. It was on this same shore where Jesus came to Peter the first time, before Peter had done anything worthy of being called, and said, "Come, follow me." And now he came to Peter even after he had messed everything up. Jesus came to Peter before Peter did anything right and even after he did everything wrong. Because that's what Jesus does.

> Shame never sleeps.
> But neither does Jesus.

Now I don't know about you, but when someone hurts me, I don't go to him or her; I expect that person to come to me. For example, when my wife, Colleen, does something that hurts or bothers me, I pull away. I back up and give her a nice long runway to come and apologize. I create a lot of relational space for her to find me and tell me how wrong she was and how amazing I am. But usually about two days go by without her apologizing. So finally I'll blurt out, "Are you going to apologize to me or what?" She'll respond with a confused look. "Apologize for what?" The problem is two days have gone by and I can't even remember why I am mad. So I'll say, "Um, I can't remember, but you were wrong and should apologize." And somehow, by the end of the argument, I end up having to apologize to her. Classic.

But even though we may pull away from one another, Jesus presses in. Jesus doesn't wait for us to come to him; he comes to us: "For the Son of Man came to seek and to save what was lost" (Luke 19:10). He finds us at our lowest points and draws us out of our hiding places, with eyes of love, hands of grace, and words of life. The good news is you don't have to look for *hope,* because *Hope* is looking for you.

READY OR NOT, HERE I COME

My kids love playing hide-and-seek. I think all kids do. Maybe it's because we are born with a propensity to hide even though we have a desire to be found. But no matter how hard my kids try, they aren't very good at hiding. As I count, they run off, attempting to disappear. But I can hear them giggling in the closet, see their toes sticking out from behind the curtains, or watch them crawl under the couch I am sitting on. Even though they try, they can't really hide from me.

We aren't kids anymore, but we still play hide-and-seek, only now it's with God. Most of us know that. We believe that he is hiding and we are seeking. We think this mysterious, elusive God is hiding somewhere way off in the cosmos and that if we search hard enough, we may get a fleeting glimpse of him. But the truth is that we are the ones who are hiding and he is the one who is seeking.

Think of Adam and Eve. As soon as they ate the forbidden fruit, they ran and hid. And so began the first game of hide-and-seek in human history. God came walking through the garden. *Adam, where are you?* Or how about Moses? After he killed a man, he ran into the desert and hid as a shepherd. God came to find Moses through the burning bush. *Moses, where are you?* What about David? After he got another man's wife pregnant and had him killed, he hid in his palace. God came to find him through the prophet Nathan. *David, where are you?*

It's the shame of failure that causes us to hide from the very love that wants to set us free. The last place we go is the first place we should run. And like little kids, we hide in plain sight while God walks through our lives whispering, *Where are you? Come out, come out, wherever you are.*

Where are you hiding? Maybe a better question is, *why* are you hiding?

God is really good at seeking. We are really bad at hiding. And he never loses.

THE ROOSTER'S CROW

"Friends, haven't you any fish?" Peter's hiding place obviously wasn't very effective. And I love how Jesus addressed him. He called him *friend*. Not sinner and loser or failure and fraud. Friend. Jesus didn't define Peter by the mess he was in. Instead, he restored his identity.

Peter's failure had damaged his view of who he was. A layer of shame was now covering him, and shame always hides truth. Jesus wanted to uncover the hidden truth by removing the sound of the rooster's crow from his mind's playlist. You know the sound: *cock-a-doodle-doo!* The voice of condemnation that plays in our minds. The voice that reminds us of our mistakes. *I'm a loser. I'm a failure. I'm unlovable. I'm a nobody. I'm worthless. I'm a mess.* What does the rooster sound like in your mind? From experience, I know he can be really loud and really mean. The crow of condemnation reminds you of what *you have done,* but the whisper of the Holy Spirit reminds you of what *Jesus has done.* Jesus silences the rooster by calling you who you are: his friend.

> Jesus got what you deserved so you could get what he deserved.

"Friends, haven't you any fish?" "No," they answered, but he already knew that. "Then throw your net over the right side of the boat." Hesitant, Peter tossed his empty net into the water, and instantly it was full of fish. Jesus overwhelmed him with kindness he didn't deserve. Talk about an unexpected twist.

Whether we realize it or not, most of us have this little religious belief in our minds that says we get what we deserve. We believe that if we *are good,* we will *receive good.* And if we *are bad,* we will *receive bad.* That's what we believe because that's what we have experienced. The world has conditioned us to believe that we get what we deserve.

Peter certainly didn't deserve a net full of fish. He deserved a hole in his boat. The story easily could read, *"Jesus comes walking down the shore. 'Hey, failures, have you caught any fish?' 'No,' they replied. 'And you're not gonna.' Jesus snaps his fingers, a hole appears in their boat, and they sink to the bottom of the sea."* We would nod our heads in agreement. "Yeah, Peter. You got what you deserved. I mean, you denied Jesus to a servant girl—come on, man." That's the gospel according to religion.

But that's not what happened. Why? Because just a few days earlier on the cross, Jesus got what Peter deserved so Peter could get what Jesus deserved. Jesus took the hole in the boat so Peter could have the net full of fish. Jesus became messy so Peter could be clean. Can you just stop for a moment and receive this truth? Jesus got what you deserved so you could get what he deserved. Your failure can't negate his love. It is no longer about what you do; it's about what he has done. Whatever mess you have created has been cleaned up by Jesus. He not only canceled your debt but also credited your account. He has forgiven your sins *and* blessed you with every spiritual blessing (see Acts 2:38; Ephesians 1:3). The net full of fish now belongs to you not because you behaved but because you believed.

DRAWN, NOT DRIVEN

When Peter realized that it was Jesus, he jumped into the water and swam to shore. The overwhelming love of God moved Peter toward Jesus. Romans 2:4 says, "God's kindness leads you toward repentance." His kindness is what frees us to step out of the darkness into the light—to bring our messes to him without fear of condemnation. When we are overwhelmed with our failure, the cloud overwhelms us with kindness. God's grace gives us favor we don't deserve and supernatural empowerment to follow. It changes our direction. It draws us forward. In the kingdom, we are drawn by grace, not driven by expectations.

We have to remember that grace draws us toward God, while shame pushes us away. Shame doesn't motivate us to follow; it drives us to our favorite hiding spots. It's a demonic tool that Satan uses to keep us trapped in darkness. Layers of shame won't change our kids, our spouses, or our friends, and it won't change us. It may motivate us to change our behavior in the moment, but it leaves us with lasting wounds. Shame hardens our hearts. That's why God never uses it and Satan always does. How different would our families and churches be if, like God, we believed that it was kindness, not shame, that changed people's hearts?

You see this with the Israelites. Even though they were constantly a stubborn and rebellious people who always wanted to go back to Egypt, God never stopped drawing them with grace:

> Because of your great compassion you did not abandon
> them in the desert. By day the pillar of cloud did not cease
> to guide them on their path, nor the pillar of fire by night
> to shine on the way they were to take. You gave your good

Spirit to instruct them. You did not withhold your manna
from their mouths, and you gave them water for their
thirst. For forty years you sustained them in the desert;
they lacked nothing, their clothes did not wear out nor did
their feet become swollen. (Nehemiah 9:19–21)

In spite of the Israelites' failures, the cloud continued provid-
ing, protecting, and guiding. God led them not because they were
good but because he was good. The cloud was the undeserved
favor of grace that opened the doors of their hearts to receive the
truth that would set them free.

There's hope for our stubborn hearts.

REMEMBER TO FORGET

I am sure that when Peter got to the shore, he was still a little
hesitant. After all, he did just deny Jesus. But graciously Jesus
invited Peter to a meal. He met Peter's needs, satisfying his hunger and thirst. Because it's only in his presence where we are
truly satisfied. And when Jesus and Peter shared this meal together, Jesus was proving what he declared on the cross—that
"it is finished" (John 19:30). He was demonstrating that there
is no more distance between God and man. There is no more
shame to drive us apart. There is no more separation between
him and us. Jesus was proving that he "will forgive their wicked-
ness and will remember their sins no more" (Hebrews 8:12).
And that "He does not treat us as our sins deserve. . . . As far as

the east is from the west, so far has he removed our transgressions from us" (Psalm 103:10, 12).

You see, the sins you can't seem to forget are the ones God can't seem to remember. The mistakes, messes, and failures you cannot get out of your mind are the ones God cannot recall. That painful divorce. That secret no one knows about. That thing you did as a teenager. Those words you wish you could take back. The things

> Jesus is always more concerned with your next step than with your misstep.

you can't forget and that you define yourself by are the things he says he can't remember. You can't out-sin the love of God. You have to stop paying for what has already been paid in full. Sometimes you need to remember to forget.

After they finished the meal, Jesus took Peter for a walk. Three times he told Peter, "Feed my sheep" (John 21:17), one for each of Peter's denials. And in that moment he restored him as a kingdom leader.

Now would you have responded to Peter that way? Would you entrust the guy who just failed you with your sheep? With your kingdom? With what you love most? Probably not. But Jesus did. And Jesus does. Jesus is always more concerned with your next step than with your misstep. Yes, Peter failed, but with Jesus no failure is fatal and no failure is final. There is always a next step. There is always a way out. It's not about what you did; it's about what you are going to do now.

Even though we often take steps that are out of alignment

with the cloud, God's grace pursues us and gets us back on track. Whether it was the Israelites, Peter, or you, God will use our failures and pain for our good and his glory (Romans 8:28; Genesis 50:20). So stop focusing on all the steps you should have or shouldn't have taken; just humbly respond to his loving correction. He promises he will restore the years, the opportunities, and the life the world has stolen from you (Joel 2:25).

Jesus knows that only his kindness can draw us to start following the cloud again. So like he did with Peter, he comes to us, restores our identity, brings us into relationship, and empowers us with purpose. That is the gospel, that is the Father's heart, and that is how the cloud leads us.

What I love maybe more than anything else in this story is what Jesus didn't do. I love what he didn't say. Nowhere in this story was there any shame or condemnation. Jesus didn't rebuke Peter with a "Try harder," "Behave better," or "You owe me" speech. Jesus wasn't preaching an angry sermon on a fishing crate, pointing his finger with judgment. Jesus doesn't do all the things we often experience in church. He does

> With Jesus no failure is fatal and no failure is final.

the unexpected and puts the love of God on display, a beautiful reminder that "there is now no condemnation for those who are in Christ Jesus" (Romans 8:1). If we spend more time talking about our failures than about his love, something is wrong. No longer is it about *our* sin, shame, and failure; it is now about *his* forgiveness, freedom, and love. His grace is always greater than our mess.

STICKY STUFF

One night, as our family was getting ready for bed, my son, Trey, who was seven at the time, was still in the kitchen packing his lunch for school. I was in our bedroom, and out of nowhere I heard the sound of shattering glass coming from the kitchen. Instantly, I knew it was bad, so I went running in. There was my son standing in a mess with huge eyes.

He cried out, "Help!"

I said, "Trey, don't move!" Quickly I put on my shoes and carried him out of the kitchen to clean him off. "Are you okay?"

"Yeah, Daddy. I'm so sorry."

I replied, "Okay, go and play and I will try to clean this up."

So I went and looked at the mess. As he had reached into the cupboard to get his snack for the next day, he accidentally knocked over a glass gallon-sized jar of maple syrup and a glass jar of coconut oil, both of which smashed on the ground and shattered into a million little glass shards. It looked as though a maple syrup bomb went off in our kitchen! (Now, the first question you should ask me is "Why do you have a gallon of maple syrup?" That is a good question, to which I have no answer.)

How do you clean that up? It was a gallon of *maple syrup!* Honestly, I am still not sure. I just started scooping it up into buckets and carrying it to the garage. And it got all over me. It got in my hair and my ears, on my clothes, and in my pockets. It was everywhere. Every time I walked back and forth between the kitchen and the garage, my shoes went *creak, creak, creak* as the sticky syrup stuck on the tile floor.

On one of my many trips back to the kitchen, I looked in the other room and saw my son, watching a movie, laughing, and having the time of his life. *Cr-ee-aa-k, cr-ee-aa-k, cr-ee-aa-k.* I gave him a little evil-eyed look as I slowly walked passed.

But when I got back to the mess, it hit me. I called out, "Trey, come here!" He came ripping around the corner expecting some punishment, by the look in his eye.

"You know how you made this mess?"

"Yeah, Daddy," he timidly replied.

"And I am cleaning it up while you are resting, playing, and laughing?"

"Yeah, Daddy."

"Well, that's exactly what Jesus does for us. We make a mess we can't clean up, and when we invite him in, he cleans it up for us while we sit and rest." I watched as the lightbulb went on in my son's heart about the simplicity of the gospel.

You see, my son couldn't have cleaned up his mess. Had he tried, he would have gotten glass shards in his hands, and maple syrup would have gotten all over everything. It would have gotten on the remote control, on his G.I. Joes, and on his pillow. We would have found it in the car, and it would have gotten on his desk at school. There was no way he could have cleaned up his mess.

That's Peter's problem. He made a mess he couldn't clean up. Shame was stuck all over him, and he couldn't get it off. If he hadn't let Jesus clean him up, everything he would have touched from that point on would have gotten the residue of shame on it. Every relationship, every activity, everywhere he went, and everything he did would have gotten the mess stuck on it. Because the mess was on him, it would have gotten on everything in his life.

The same is true for us. We make a mess we can't clean up. And if we don't let Jesus clean us up, everything we touch gets the sin and shame stuck on it. It gets on our jobs, relationships, marriages, kids, activities, hobbies, finances, purposes, church lives, and so on. Why? Because the mess is in our hearts, so everything we touch is affected. Sometimes we wonder, *Why are my finances always a mess? Why is my marriage always a mess? Why is my life always a mess?* It's because there is a mess in our hearts.

But whenever we cry out "Help," Jesus comes to do for us what we could never do for ourselves: "God made him who had no sin to be sin for us, so that in him we might become the righteousness of God" (2 Corinthians 5:21). In other words, Jesus became messy so we could become clean. He took our messes upon himself. He was condemned so we don't have to be. The wrath of God was poured out on Jesus so the love of God could be poured out on us. And it's in our moments of greatest failure where his love is most clearly seen. It's in the moments where we knock over the jars of maple syrup, when we have left our spouses, done those things we swore we'd never do, made those mistakes (again), or had darkness in our hearts—where his kindness overwhelms our lives.

The truth is, John 21 is really our story. Like Peter, we fail and spend our lives trying to hide our messes. Peter hid in a fishing boat. Where are you hiding? No matter where it may be, the resurrected Jesus comes walking down the shore of your life and doesn't say, "Hey, sinner/loser/failure/fraud." He doesn't call you by all the names the rooster does. He doesn't even call you by the names you call yourself.

He says, "Hey, *friend*. Have you caught any fish?" In essence, "Have you found what you are looking for?"

We say, "No."

He says, "Then throw your net over the right side of the boat." And he overwhelms us with kindness, draws us into his presence, empowers us with purpose, and redeems the lives God created for us to live. The cloud leads us out of our failures to discover who we really are.

Follow the Cloud—Live Free

All of us are pretty good at hiding. What are two areas in your life where you are hiding right now? Why are you hiding? How is God's kindness trying to draw you out from your favorite hiding place?

We all make mistakes and create messes in our lives. What's your current "Jesus, help me" mess? Are you trying to clean it up by yourself or are you inviting him in? How do you hope he will respond to your call for help? Why do you believe that?

5

BECOMING WHO WE ALREADY ARE

Several years ago, on our way to school one morning, my five-year-old daughter, Emma Joy, had her favorite doll, Isabelle, with her. Playfully, I said, "Hey, baby, how is *Samantha* today?" "Daddy, her name is Isabelle, not Samantha." A few minutes later, I said, "Is Samantha ready for a big day?" Annoyed, Emma replied, "Daddy, her name is not Samantha." Now, I know I was pushing it, but one more time I said, "Hey, does Samantha have her backpack for school?" And from the backseat of my truck, I heard this giant roar come out of this little girl: "Daddy, her name is not Samantha, it's Isabelle. She is my doll. She belongs to me, and only I get to say who she is. Her name is Isabelle!"

I have never called Isabelle *Samantha* again.

That day, the childlike faith of my little girl echoed a profound truth: whoever owns you gets to define you. As I drove home after dropping her and Isabelle off, I kept thinking about those words. *You're mine. You belong to me. And only I get to say who you are.*

Can I ask you a really simple question? Who, or what, gets to say who you are? Put differently, where does your identity come from? Maybe it's from the names your dad called you when you were a kid. Maybe it's from what your ex has said about you. Maybe it's from the job title you have worked really hard for. Maybe your identity has come from where you have been, what you have done, the possessions you have, the awards you've won, the mistakes you've made, or the struggles you've endured. Although all of those things may have shaped you in some way, they don't define you. And if they do define you, it's because you have allowed them to.

> Whoever owns you gets to define you.

I love what God says to Jeremiah:

"Before I formed you in the womb I knew you,
    before you were born I set you apart;
    I appointed you as a prophet to the nations."

"Ah, Sovereign Lord," I said, "I do not know how to speak; I am only a child."

But the Lord said to me, *"Do not say 'I am only a child.'* You must go to everyone I send you to and say whatever I command you. Do not be afraid of them, for I am with you and will rescue you." (Jeremiah 1:5–8).

What God told Jeremiah, God tells us: *Hey, I formed you, I know you, I set you apart, and I appointed you. You belong to me, so only I get to say who you are.* God is reminding us that only his voice has the authority to declare our identity. You aren't who *they* say you are. You aren't even who *you* say you are. You are who *he* says you are. In other words, when God tells you who you are, don't tell him who you are not. When God calls you a prophet, don't call yourself a child. When God calls you beloved, don't say you're unlovable. When God says you're strong, don't let anyone say you're weak. If he calls you victorious, don't let anyone say you're defeated. If God declares he is well pleased with you, don't say you're a disappointment. Maybe it's time to start agreeing with what the Author of Truth has declared. Whoever owns you gets to define you.

There is a continual roar from heaven declaring, *"You're mine. You belong to me. And only I get to say who you are."* Can you hear it?

Restored

Too often we ignore the roar and allow something else to define us. In fact, broken identity is the plague of humanity. When Adam sinned, he not only got us kicked out of the garden but he fractured our identity. He made us guilty, and he also made us ashamed. We lost who we *were,* and now we spend our lives trying to discover, define, and cover up who we *are.*

Everywhere we look, we see people struggling to find their identity: the workaholic who is never home, the student who is sleeping around, the victim who never leaves, the woman consumed with her looks. A lot of the behaviors that we are confused by, or judge, in others are really just an overflow of a shattered identity.

But what Adam lost, Jesus came to restore.

"Just as through the disobedience of the one man the many were made sinners, so also through the obedience of the one man the many will be made righteous" (Romans 5:19). Adam's disobedience changed our identity and made us sinners. His actions trapped us in a prison of sin we couldn't get ourselves out of. In Adam, we aren't sinners because we sin; we sin because we are sinners. Sinner isn't what we did; it was who we were.

But now, through Jesus's obedience, we have been made righteous. His action, not ours, rescued us from the prison of sin and set us free in his righteousness. *Righteousness* is a big word that simply means right standing with God. It means we are fully restored. Jesus cleansed us from sin, healed our brokenness, and gave us back our purpose. He changed our identity. In Jesus, we are no longer defined as sinners; *we are righteous.*

In fact, there is no such thing as a righteous sinner. You can't be righteous and a sinner at the same time, because no one can have two identities. You are either righteous or a sinner. You are either under the redemption of Jesus or still under the curse of Adam. You are either a new creation or you are not (see 2 Corinthians 5:17). There is no in between. So when God says you are righteous, don't tell him you are a sinner. Whoever you believe you are will determine how you live. If you believe you are a sinner, then by faith you will live a life of sin. But if you believe you are righteous, then by faith you will live righteously. Identity determines behavior, because you do who you are.

GRACE CHANGES EVERYTHING

It's interesting to me how much we resist this truth. If we are honest, this is often beyond our Christian comfort zone. I remember meeting with a guy, let's call him Bill, who was leaving our church because he said I didn't preach enough about sin. He was tired of hearing about the resurrection life. He passionately told me, "I am a sinner, and I want to be reminded of that every week so I don't stop following Jesus." Unfortunately, he believed that hearing about his sin, instead of hearing about God's forgiveness, would empower him to follow Jesus. And although condemnation might lead to short-term behavior modification, it creates long-term hardening of our hearts.

Just think about this for a moment. Does someone with an alcohol problem quit drinking by being called an alcoholic? Does a person who struggles with lying start telling the truth because he or she has been shamed as a liar? Does someone who is addicted to pornography quit looking at the screen through condemnation? No. That just reinforces a false identity. We change by receiving God's grace.

> Although condemnation might lead to short-term behavior modification, it creates long-term hardening of our hearts.

Jesus says to us what he said to the woman caught in adultery: "Neither do I condemn you; go and sin no more" (John 8:11, NKJV). Sin loses its power when we realize that it no longer defines us. Like many of us, Bill had a misunderstanding of the gospel.

He had a false view of his identity and found comfort in being defined by his mistakes. He was allowing his sin to have more authority over his life than the Cross and Resurrection. But the fact is, in Jesus, *he is no longer a sinner; he is righteous.* Yes, Bill might still sin—a lot. But just as his good deeds couldn't change his identity and make him righteous (see Ephesians 2:8–9), his mistakes can't change his identity back and make him a sinner.

Sadly, a lot of us live trapped in this thinking. It sounds really spiritual to define ourselves as sinners just barely saved by grace. If religious points were given out to those who live with a self-demeaning perspective, some of us would have a platinum status. Em-

> Doesn't it take more faith to believe that we are now defined by what *Jesus did* instead of what *we do*?

ulating the negative attitude of Eeyore, we often walk around mumbling, "Ohhhhhhh, well, I guess I'll always be a sinner." While that may sound holy, the problem is that it takes no faith. I know we mean well and want to please God, but we need to think higher. Yes, we *were* sinners, and we might still struggle with sin. But we *have been* saved by grace, which means we *now are* righteous.

Don't you think God is pleased when we call ourselves his beloved sons and daughters instead of worthless sinners? Isn't it more honoring to believe that we are completely forgiven even when we are aware of our current failures? Doesn't it take more faith to believe that we are now defined by what *Jesus did* instead of what *we do*? Humility is not putting ourselves down; it's agreeing with who God says we are.

Remember, "without faith it is impossible to please God" (Hebrews 11:6). So if we really want to please God, we should start believing what he has said about who we are in Jesus. It takes faith to believe that we are who he says we are, especially when it contradicts how we feel. But God's truth is always superior to our feelings. Yes, we still sin, but our failures no longer define who we are. "Sin is no longer your master, for you no longer live under the requirements of the law. Instead, you live under the freedom of God's grace" (Romans 6:14, NLT). Because sin is no longer our master, it no longer gets to define us. We are more than sinners saved by grace; we are beloved sons and daughters.

FEELING GUILTY

I don't know about you, but I grew up in what I call a "sin-focused church." When I say sin-focused church, I'm referring to a church that has more faith in the power of sin than in the power of Jesus, a church that is more focused on what we have to do for him than on what he has done for us, a church that lives on the wrong side of the Cross. So I always left feeling guilty. But if we leave church feeling worse than when we came, something is wrong, because the kingdom is "righteousness, peace and joy" (Romans 14:17). And although the people there loved me and had good intentions, some of their focus was misplaced. Sadly, I think there are a lot of churches like this.

Everything from the messages to the conversations, from the flannelgraphs to the hymns, were built around the power of sin and the failure of man. It was a continual reminder that we were sinners just barely saved by grace serving an angry God. I must have gotten "saved" at least a thousand times. Every time there was an altar call, I responded because I was terrified the Rapture would happen and I would be left behind. I grew up believing that I could lose fellowship with God, that he was disappointed in me, and that he was going to "get me" when I messed up. I am sure there was some hope sprinkled in there, but all I can remember was the continual reminder that I was a sinner. That is who I was. That is who I would always be. It was the constant reinforcement of a false identity, which created a life of striving. I believed in Jesus, but I still thought my behavior determined who I was. And that is an exhausting way to live.

Unfortunately, all that talk about sin didn't change my behavior much. It just left me feeling distant from God. As you might expect, I grew up with a pretty skewed view of who God *really* is and who I *really* am.

Maybe you can relate.

The problem with this kind of thinking is that it leaves you hopelessly trapped. And although it may sound good, it keeps you enslaved to an already-defeated enemy. If life is always about managing your sin, how do you ever live in the freedom of God's love? How do you follow a God who you believe is always disappointed in you? I am not sure you really can. In fact, if sin management is the focus of our lives, we are in danger of living drastically inferior lives to what Jesus offers us.

STARTING AT THE FINISH

Let me try to explain this to you the way I wish someone would have explained it me.

When Jesus breathed his last breath on the cross, he declared the most significant words of all time: *It is finished!* Finished. Complete. Done. Nothing left to do. No more separation. No more shame. And no more striving. Our identity has been established. *We start at his finish.* God has gone to great lengths to help us believe that we start following the cloud from where Jesus left off.

Under the Old Covenant, or the Law, God basically said, "If you obey me, then I will bless you." If you did the right things, then you would have God's favor. It was conditional acceptance, and your behavior was the focus. Just look at the Ten Commandments. *You shall* not commit adultery. *You shall* not murder. *You shall* not steal. *You shall*—the focus was on you and your effort. You had to achieve God's favor.

A lot of us still live this way, often subconsciously, and it looks something like this: *If I _____, then he will _____. If I go to church, then maybe he will give me that promotion. If I give some money, then maybe he will heal my loved one. If I serve someone, then maybe he will fix my marriage.* Or, out of fear, we do the inverse. *I better not sin this week so he will help me pass this test, get this job, or receive a good doctor's report.* Old Covenant thinking leaves us in a constant state of wondering where we stand with God. And if you struggle at all like I do, you understand that this is not good news.

But under the New Covenant, or grace, God says, "Because of what I have done, I will bless you." The focus is no longer on what we have to do; it is on what Jesus has done. His finished work has released the unending favor of God into our lives. We live by his efforts, not ours. "This righteousness from God comes through faith in Jesus Christ to all who believe" (Romans 3:22). Instead of achieving, we now live by receiving. Grace provides what the Law demands. Jesus fulfilled all that ever has been or will be required of us. There are no sacrifices left to offer. All we have to do is, by faith, believe that he is who he says he is and did what he said he did. Instead of *you shall*, it's *he has*.

God says we are now seated with him because we rest in the finished work of Jesus. "Because of his great love for us, God, who is rich in mercy, made us alive with Christ even when we were dead in transgressions—it is by grace you have been saved. And God raised us up with Christ and seated us with him in the heavenly realms in Christ Jesus" (Ephesians 2:4–6).

Did you catch that? We're seated because there's no work left to do. We enjoy the fruit of his labor. There is nothing to prove. There is nothing to add. There is nothing to earn. It's already yours. The heavenly realm is not our destination; it's our starting place.

Religion starts by putting burdens on us; Jesus starts by taking burdens off of us. Instead of "sin-focused church," maybe we need "Jesus-focused church." Let's not take the *good* out of the good news. Our unwillingness to receive the fullness of salvation has cost us dearly. Jesus said, "It is finished," not "I'm working on it." His finish line is our starting point. The more we believe we are fully forgiven, the more we are drawn to courageously take each next step he gives us.

REMOVE AND REPLACE

As we have learned to receive the finished work of Jesus at Valley Creek, it has helped us discover the simple truth that identity always determines behavior. Who you are determines what you do. Fish swim, birds fly, cows moo, dogs bark, sinners sin, and righteous people live righteously. I love how simple and yet profound that is. Our behavior is always a direct result of who we believe we are. That is why a little boy who believes he is a superhero acts as if he has superpowers, runs around in a costume, and thinks he can do impossible feats. It's why a little girl who believes she is a princess acts like she is royalty, has tea parties, and expects everyone to obey her commands. Who we believe we are determines what we do.

So if you want to know who you believe you are, just look at your behavior. It is a direct reflection of what you actually believe about yourself. For example, if you are constantly performing,

> Identity always determines behavior.

maybe it's because you believe you are unworthy. If you are continually people pleasing, maybe it's because you believe you are unlovable. If you are always busy, maybe it's because you believe you are insignificant. What does your behavior reveal about who you believe you are?

A misunderstanding of your identity will ultimately steal

your purpose and destroy your destiny. Just look at the Israelites. Instead of seeing themselves as God's empowered children, they had an ungodly belief and saw themselves as insignificant grasshoppers. "The land we explored devours those living in it. All the people we saw there are of great size. . . . *We seemed like grasshoppers in our own eyes,* and we looked the same to them. . . . We should choose a leader and go back to Egypt" (Numbers 13:32–33; 14:4). Grasshoppers don't fight giants, but God's children do. The Israelites allowed themselves to be defined by their perspective instead of God's, and it cost them everything—forty years of wandering the desert.

> Repentance frees you to become who you already are in Jesus.

Unfortunately, wrong thinking will never lead to right living. And it's impossible to have a big faith with a small identity.

So maybe we need to change our perspective.

While Christianity is often focused on behavior modification, God is focused on identity declaration. He knows that who you believe you are will determine what you do. The wrong root will never produce the right fruit. So while we try to change how people *behave,* God tries to change what people *believe.*

That is why Jesus's main message was "Repent, for the kingdom of heaven is near" (Matthew 4:17). The word *repent* literally means to change your mind. Jesus was saying, "Change your thinking because a superior reality is here." In other words, if you want to change how you live, you need to agree with who he says you now are. He wants you to repent so you can remove the lies and replace them with his truth—to come into agreement with what he has said, regardless of how you feel. Repentance frees you to become who you already are in Jesus.

A GREAT DISCOVERY

A great example of this is the story of Gideon. "The LORD is with you, mighty warrior" (Judges 6:12). I am sure those words were shocking to Gideon. No one had ever referred to him as a mighty anything, except maybe a mighty loser. Gideon defined himself by his weakness. "My clan is the weakest . . . and I am the least in my family" (verse 15). So he spent his life hiding, threshing wheat in a winepress.

Now I don't know much about wheat, but I am pretty sure it's not threshed in a winepress. It's a great reminder that when we don't know who we are, we'll always spend our lives doing the wrong things. But even though Gideon was hiding in his favorite hiding place, God found him and called him a mighty warrior. The moment God spoke, Gideon's identity was established, because whoever owns you gets to define you. "Go in the strength you have and save Israel out of Midian's hand. Am I not sending you?" (verse 14). God declared Gideon's identity and then gave him a next step to discover it. God didn't need Gideon to defeat the Midianites; Gideon needed this next step to discover who he already was. Only in following God would he become who God said he already was. So full of fear, Gideon took his next step, destroyed the Midianites, and discovered he had believed a lie about his identity. He was never *the least;* he had always been *a mighty warrior.*

For the past few years, I have watched almost every one of our staff team members go through a similar process of uncovering their true identity. Becca, for example, had a great career as an airline executive, until one day the cloud started to move. Like Gideon, she had been threshing wheat in a winepress by trying to use success to define her worth. But God had better plans. He invited her to take a next step and become a nursery-preschool pastor. Talk about change. From boardrooms to nursery rooms. From conference tables to changing tables.

At first she rationalized the move and believed she was doing something great for God. But as the journey unfolded, she realized God was doing something great for her. With each next step, he was helping her discover who she had always been. He was giving her a revelation of her identity that she had never had before: his beloved daughter who had nothing to prove, nothing to earn, and nothing to achieve. She was free to live with a whole heart. Lies that defined her identity were replaced with his truth. No longer was she defined by her title, accomplishments, victories or failures; she was defined by his love. She started to become who she already was, a discovery she couldn't have made on her own—a discovery you can't make on your own.

The same God who called fearful Gideon a mighty warrior, childless Abraham a father, and shaky Peter a rock calls you who you are and then gives you a next step so you can discover it for yourself.

Next steps aren't expectations to fulfill; they are discoveries to be made.

Remember that in Jesus your identity is already established. There is nothing you can do to add to or take away from it. All you can do is discover it. That is why we take next steps and follow the cloud. Our motive of following God is not to earn something from him but rather to discover the fullness of what we already have in him. Remember, we are drawn by grace, not driven by expectations. We don't take next steps to *become* someone; we take next steps because we *are* someone. We don't obey God to *earn* his favor; we obey him because we *have* his favor. We don't follow the cloud to *find* significance; we follow the cloud because we *are* significant. Every next step we take helps us discover more of who we already are. And if we refuse that step, God isn't disappointed in us, we don't lose fellowship with him, and he isn't going to "get us." We just won't uncover the true versions of ourselves.

Which brings us back to the Israelites. God brought them out of Egypt, but he needed to get Egypt out of them. They were the children of God, but they still lived like slaves. So everywhere the cloud led them was designed to expose their old way of thinking and help them discover more of their new identity. Whether it was water from the rock, manna from heaven, resting on the Sabbath, or fighting battles, each step was an opportunity to change their thinking and discover who they already were. That is why God

> We don't take next steps to *become* someone; we take next steps because we *are* someone. We don't obey God to *earn* his favor; we obey him because we *have* his favor. We don't follow the cloud to *find* significance; we follow the cloud because we *are* significant.

was always reminding them, "I am the LORD your God, who brought you out of Egypt so that you would no longer be slaves to the Egyptians; I broke the bars of your yoke and enabled you to walk with heads held high" (Leviticus 26:13). He would point back to their salvation to remind them that he had already established their identity. All they had to do was believe it.

The same is true for us. The Holy Spirit is always pointing us to the finished work of the Cross to remind us that he has already established our identity. The problem is that our old identity has programmed our thinking. In Jesus we are righteous, but we still think like sinners. Sometimes old habits die hard.

So with every step God asks you to take, he is reprogramming your thinking and helping you discover more of who you already are. Whether it's giving something up, serving someone, doing something that seems impossible, or raising your hands in worship, each step helps you uncover your true identity.

You become who you already are when you simply follow by faith. With each step you take, you'll start to discover that in Jesus:

- *You are already loved—which means you have nothing to fear.*
- *You are already forgiven—which means you have no debt to pay.*
- *You are already his masterpiece—which means you are valuable.*
- *You are already free—which means nothing can hold you back.*

- *You are already accepted—which means you have nothing to prove.*
- *You are already his beloved son or daughter—which means you are alive!*

The roar from heaven says, *"You're mine. You belong to me. And only I get to say who you are."*

Mighty warrior, it's time to become who you already are.

Follow the Cloud—Live Free

Challenge: Tweet your identity. More specifically, write who you are in 140 characters or less. Now look carefully at what you wrote. Where have you allowed the voices of this world, the shame of your past, or the accomplishments of your hands to define who you believe you are?

Repentance is the process of changing your thinking and choosing to come into agreement with God. Where do you need to repent in regard to your identity? What lies need to be removed and replaced with God's truth? Take a moment and ask the Holy Spirit who he says you are. Write those identity statements on your phone's home screen or on sticky notes for your bathroom mirror. Declare them every day for a month.

6

BELOVED SONS AND DAUGHTERS

There is a carved wooden sign that hangs over the desk in my office that reads, "Beloved Son." It is a constant reminder of who I am. Every time I sit there, I allow that truth to wash over me because I never want to go back to how I used to live.

That sign is so meaningful to me because there used to be another sign that was carved on the door of my heart. That sign read, "No one wants me for me; they want me for what I can do." It's sad to admit, but that was the lie I believed for most of my life. It was a lie that I was completely unaware of but one that defined almost every aspect of my life. I believed that my value came from what I could do, not who I was. And whenever you believe a lie you give authority to the Liar.

For years, I had unknowingly empowered the Liar to enslave me to a life of performance. I performed in school. I performed in lacrosse. I performed in work. I performed in my relationships. I performed as a pastor. And I nailed it. I won championships, collected awards, and achieved great accomplishments all at a young

age. But nothing ever filled the cracks in my heart. I used success
to hide my insecurities. I thought, *If you love me for what I can
do, then I have to keep performing so you will keep me around.*
Unfortunately, the problem with performance is that it leads to
more performance. The more you perform, the more you have to
keep performing. And that is an exhausting way to live.

Ultimately, I performed for others because deep down I believed I had to perform for God. I believed that God didn't want
me for me but rather for what I could do, so I was a slave trapped
in my own life. Maybe you know how that feels.

But Jesus said, "Then you will know the truth, and the truth
will set you free" (John 8:32). The truth is that Jesus didn't die so
we could become God's slaves; he died so we could become God's
children. While Satan wants slaves, God wants sons and daughters. And the difference between the two is that slaves perform,
while sons receive. Slaves have to perform to prove their value and
worth to the world, but sons receive love and affirmation from
their Father.

Sadly, many of us perform like a slave without even realizing
it. Like Martha, we are busy making meals Jesus never ordered
(Luke 10:38–42). Like the older brother in the prodigal son story,
we try to earn a love that's already ours (Luke

> Life isn't about how much we achieve; it's about how well we receive.

15:11–32). Religion tells us to run higher and jump faster (yes, run
higher and jump faster, which is impossible). So we continue to try
harder, behave better, and do more, all in an attempt to become

someone, not realizing that we have gotten the three circles—the gospel—backward. We spend our lives striving to behave in order to become. But no matter how much we accomplish, it never brings us the significance we are looking for. It's easy to try to find our worth in our caregiving, beauty, success, status, and titles. But life isn't about how much we achieve; it's about how well we receive. "To all who received him, to those who believed in his name, he gave the right to become children of God" (John 1:12).

It's time to break the lie.

BECAUSE HE IS, SO AM I

I love baptisms (as long as I am not baptizing a guy who's six foot seven). They are defining moments in our lives. I love watching people share their stories and, by faith, go into the water. As they go under, their old lives are washed away and they come up to the new lives they have in Jesus.

I wish I could have watched Jesus's baptism, as it was a defining moment for humanity. "When He had been baptized, Jesus came up immediately from the water; and behold, the heavens were opened to Him, and He saw the Spirit of God descending like a dove and alighting upon Him. And suddenly a voice came from heaven, saying, 'This is My beloved Son, in whom I am well pleased'" (Matthew 3:16–17, NKJV). When Jesus was baptized, the Father declared his identity because only the Father has the authority to define who we are. The Father said that Jesus was his beloved Son, in whom he was well pleased.

Now, think about this for a minute. This was the beginning

of Jesus's ministry. He hadn't done anything yet. He hadn't healed any sick people, cast out any demons, raised anyone from the dead, performed any miracles, or achieved anything, yet the Father was well pleased in him. The Father was well pleased in Jesus not because of what he did but because of who he was. And this declaration was the source of Jesus's security.

Do you realize that if we are now "in Jesus," this is true of us as well? First John 4:17 says, "As He is, so are we in this world" (NKJV). Jesus is not a picture of who I can become; he is a mirror of who I now am. He isn't a picture of what I can someday become if I try really hard; he is a mirror of who I already am, and the more I look to him, the more I discover who I now am (see 2 Corinthians 3:18). We don't change by trying harder; we change by looking at Jesus. Because he is, so am I. Because he is righteous, so am I. Because he is loved, so am I. Because he is victorious, so am I. *As he is, so are we.*

So like Jesus, you are the Father's beloved son or daughter, in whom he is well pleased. This means that before you do anything, he is well pleased in you because of Jesus. You don't have to earn through performance what you have now received by grace. Your heart was created to need the approval of the Father, and you already have it. How different would our lives be if we believed that in Jesus we are already accepted, loved, significant, and secure?

This simple and profound truth is why Jesus walked in complete freedom. Everywhere he went, the world tried to define him. They called him Beelzebub (see Mark 3:22), a deceiver, crazy, and demon possessed, yet Jesus never defended himself. Now, I'm just saying, if you call me Beelzebub, we're going to have some words. But not Jesus. He never had the need to justify, validate, or prove himself to the world. Why? Because when the Father calls you a beloved son, no one can tell you you're not. Security comes from the Father's love, and secure people have no need to perform for anyone. They have nothing to prove because they know who they are, which means they are free to follow the cloud regardless of what anyone else thinks.

THE ULTIMATE CLOUD FOLLOWER

If we want to know what it looks like to follow the cloud, Jesus's life is a much better example than the lives of the Israelites. He tells us that he only did what he saw the Father doing, went where he saw the Father going, and said what he heard the Father saying. He lived from the invitation of the Father, not the response of people. In other words, he was the ultimate cloud follower. He believed in the goodness of his Father, and he knew he was a beloved son. And beloved sons inherently trust their Father. He knew that the cloud was drawn by the Father's love, not driven by the winds of chance, so he took every next step the Father gave him.

Jesus's willingness to receive the love of the Father allowed him to follow the cloud to places few of us ever go and to experience a life few of us ever do. He knew that life was found wherever the Father was leading him—that home is not a place to be discovered but a love to be received. He trusted the Father's heart enough to walk out into the storm, touch a contagious leper, leave the crowd that wanted to make him king, be born in a manger, and surrender to the cross. Jesus understood that it's only in complete trust that we find complete freedom.

Even though people were constantly putting demands and expectations on him, he did only what the Father asked him to do. He wasn't drawn to the praise of man, so he wasn't defeated by the rejection of man. Jesus didn't need from people what he already had in the Father. He could follow the cloud into any situation, and whether he was received or rejected, he left the same because he knew he was loved and had nothing to prove.

Sadly, a lot of us never really start *following the cloud* because we are too busy *chasing the crowd*. Instead of living by the invitation of the Father, we often live by the response of people—trying to meet their demands and expectations, trying to get their affirmation and approval. But if you need the praise of man you will always be defeated by the rejection of man. If you need people to celebrate you, you will be destroyed when they criticize you. But you don't need from people what you already have in the Father. That is

> A lot of us never really start *following the cloud* because we are too busy *chasing the crowd*.

the freedom of being a beloved son or daughter.

Can you imagine for a moment if Jesus was constantly posting selfies? He could have captured some killer shots: *Here's me walking on water #whoneedsaboat? Here's me with Moses and Elijah #meandtheboys. Here's me raising a little girl from the dead #Igotthis.* That just sounds ridiculous, doesn't it? Jesus joyfully remained hidden because he had no need to announce himself to the world. He didn't need anyone to *like* his status, because he *knew* his status. He received security in the quiet place with the Father, not from the affirmation of the crowd. "If I testify about myself, my testimony is not valid. There is another who *testifies* in my favor, and *I know* that his testimony about me is valid" (John 5:31–32). Jesus said that the Father testified about him and that was enough. He lived *from* the Father's approval, not *for* it.

So here are some things to ask yourself: Who do you need to testify about you? Yourself? Your boss? Your spouse? Your industry? Your friends? Do you need others to say you are pretty, successful, or cool? What are you trying to prove, and who are you trying to prove it to? Jesus has already proved it for you. In him, you are the Father's beloved son or daughter, in whom he is well pleased, and that *is* enough. When the Father testifies about you, no one else has to. And notice it says *testifies,* not *testified,* which means the Father is *continually* giving you his affirmation and approval. Don't waste your life trying to get the world to say what the Father already has: *you are loved.*

You Are Beloved

Other than salvation, this revelation has changed my life more than anything else. As I have learned to receive this truth for myself, it has freed me from so many of the struggles I have dealt with since childhood. God's truth changes how we live. But it hasn't come easy. I have discovered that whenever your identity is declared, it will always be tested. Just look at Jesus.

When the Father said, "This is my beloved Son," the Spirit immediately led him into the wilderness, where Satan tempted him: "If you are the Son of God, tell these stones to become bread" (Matthew 4:3). Three times Satan tempted Jesus to prove his identity in different ways. But notice that he left out the most important word: *beloved*. This wasn't a simple oversight; it was a strategic attack. Satan will never remind you that you are loved because love makes you fearless. "There is no fear in love. But perfect love drives out fear, because fear has to do with punishment. The one who fears is not made perfect in love" (1 John 4:18). The Father's love makes you free. It drives out your fears and fills you with courage. Love gives you the hope and the faith to follow.

Satan doesn't care if you know you are a son or daughter; he cares when you know you are a *beloved* son or daughter. He knows that if he reminds you that you are loved, you won't fall to temptation. He knows that when you believe you are loved, you won't hide from the Father but run directly to him. He knows that in the Father's love you have everything you will ever need. Satan can't stop you from being loved, but he will do everything he can to keep you from believing that you are.

> Satan will never remind you that you are loved because love makes you fearless.

COMING HOME

One of our culture's great lies is that freedom is found in independence. We have bought into the trap that a lack of authority would make us completely free. If only I could do what I want, when I want, and how I want, then I would be free. That is the lie Adam and Eve believed. They believed freedom was found in being on their own instead of under the care of the Father, so they traded in sonship for an orphan lifestyle. Satan offered them slavery disguised as freedom. He tricked them into pursuing in the world what they already had in the Father. And we have been doing the same thing ever since. But true freedom is not found in independence; it is found in submission to a good Father.

Take my kids, for example. They are the freest people I know. They have absolutely no control or independence. They are in complete submission to me as their dad—at least most of the time. Their lives are defined by laughter, joy, peace, provision, trust, hope, and love. They run around our house singing, dancing, and playing games. Their biggest stress is deciding what toys they should play with. My kids are fully known, fully loved, with no fear of rejection. They live as a beloved son and daughter.

Now compare that to many of the adults you know. They control their time, money, and life. They live in complete independence, yet they are some of the most enslaved people you will ever meet. Stress, fear, anger, hoarding, bitterness, striving, performing, and loneliness define their lives. They aren't really known by anyone, they don't believe they are loved, and they live with constant fear of rejection. They live as orphans.

The difference between a son or daughter and a spiritual orphan is simply the willingness to receive the love of the Father. The Father is your source of life. He gives you your name and identity.

He gives you safety and protection. He gives you provision and value. He gives you purpose and direction. He gives you freedom.

The problem, though, is that most of us resist the Father. The fundamental wounding of humanity is the orphaned heart. It's a fatherless existence where we believe we are on our own. The consequence of sin has caused us to prefer to live as orphans, because to live as sons requires trust. And we would rather have control than dependence. Unfortunately, that leaves us trying to make names for ourselves, validate our significance, cover our shame, provide for our needs, and prove our worth. Without the love of the Father we are afraid to open ourselves up to receive and give love. Sadly, the orphan heart never feels at home anywhere. And when we never feel at home, we can never be at rest. Maybe our restless society is simply the result of our orphaned hearts.

This is a partial list of what our hearts look like without and with the love of the Father.

Spiritual Orphans	Beloved Sons and Daughters
See God as Master	See God as Father
Live with fear	Live in freedom
Take care of themselves	Allow themselves to be loved
Feel lonely	Feel wanted and accepted
Live independently	Live completely dependent
Achieve and perform	Receive and rest
Have a poverty mind-set	Have an abundance mind-set
Tend to be skeptical	Fully trust

So can I ask you, which of those sound more like your life? Is your life defined by the freedom of singing and dancing or by the bondage of fear and anxiety?

> When we never feel at home, we can never be at rest.

You don't have to be an orphan anymore. "I will not leave you as orphans; I will come to you" (John 14:18).

Jesus has come to the orphanage of this world to bring us home.

THE PATHWAY TO HEALING

As I have talked with my friends who have adopted children, I have learned that the transition from orphan to son or daughter isn't as easy as we might think. The stories they have told me are often eerily similar and look something like this.

Loving parents go to an orphanage in a foreign land and rescue a child out of heartbreaking conditions. They change the child's identity, give him or her a new name, and bring them into a loving home. But just because the child has been adopted doesn't mean he knows how to live in the freedom of love. The parents are shocked when they find the child hiding food in the closet or under the bed. They are confused when the child refuses to share toys with the other children in the family. They don't understand why the child refuses to receive affection and lashes out in anger. Sadly, orphan living is still possible even in a loving family.

In the orphanage, the child never knew when she would be

fed again, so she learned to hide food in order to survive. He discovered that every time he gave away something, perhaps a toy, he would never get it back. And the only interaction they had with adults was full of rejection and pain so they were unwilling to get close to anyone. My friends have told me how they have had to show the child the kitchen cupboard and say, "You see all this? This is all yours and you can have as much as want. You see these toys? These belong to our family and you can play with them anytime. You feel this hug and kiss? No matter what you do, we will never stop hugging and kissing you for the rest of your life."

> There's a big difference between being set free and living free.

Even though these children have been adopted as beloved sons and daughters, they still think like orphans. They have been conditioned by years of orphan living and don't know how to think or live in love. But just because they behave like orphans doesn't mean they aren't beloved sons and daughters.

The same is true with us. We are not orphans anymore. We have been adopted as beloved sons and daughters. "You did not receive a spirit that makes you a slave again to fear, but you received the Spirit of sonship. And by him we cry, '*Abba,* Father.' The Spirit himself testifies with our spirit that we are God's children" (Romans 8:15–16). But there's a big difference between being set free and living free.

We have lived in the orphanage of this world for so long that we still think like spiritual orphans. We hide, hoard, and hate. So the Father opens the cupboard of heaven and says, "You see all this? Everything I have now belongs to you." The Father points to Jesus and reminds us that "he who did not spare his own Son, but gave him up for us all—how will he not also, along with him, graciously give us all things?" (verse 32). The Father essentially says, "If I gave you my best—Jesus—don't you think I will give you everything else?"

The problem is like that of the Israelites: we struggle to see God as loving Father because we are so used to the taskmaster of this world. So God invites us on a journey to change the way we think. Following the cloud was an invitation for the Israelites to learn how to live in the freedom of the Father's love, and that is the same invitation we have today.

If the kingdom of heaven belongs to little children, then every next step is the pathway to healing our orphaned hearts. To follow the cloud is to trust in the Father's heart. And it's time to come home.

HE'S NOT LIKE YOUR DAD

I am not sure what you think when you hear the word *father*. A lot of us have an unhealthy view of what a father is because of the wounds we carry from our earthly fathers. As adults, we resist God as Father because our fathers have hurt us. We have been abandoned, rejected, abused, and mistreated when what we needed was to be loved, affirmed, valued, and protected. Our hearts have cried, *See me! Notice me! Want me! Believe in me! Am I pretty? Am I strong? Do I have what it takes?*

We have a hard time believing that we are loved and pleasing because very few of our fathers ever told us that we were. In fact, some of you have been so hurt by your dad that you are having a hard time even reading this chapter. But your dad is not the image of the Father; Jesus is.

Jesus said, "Anyone who has seen me has seen the Father" (John 14:9). Simply put, Jesus is the exact representation of the Father. He is the image and likeness of who the Father is. If you want to know what the Father is like, don't look at your dad; look at Jesus. The Father comforts like Jesus comforts, loves like Jesus loves, cares like Jesus cares, heals like Jesus heals. He has the same tenderness, kindness, and faithfulness that Jesus has. The goodness you see in Jesus is the goodness of the Father being revealed to us. Jesus came to show us what the Father is really like in a world full of broken father figures.

The reason there are so many broken father figures is because orphans can never truly become fathers; only sons can. You have to be fathered before you can become a father. You have to receive as a son or daughter before you can raise sons and daughters. Because you can give only what you have received (see Matthew 10:8). And since many of our father figures haven't received the love of the Father, they are unable to give us the love of a father. They hurt us because they themselves are hurting. Hurting people hurt people. They couldn't give you the love they never had. But don't let the pain from your hurting earthly father keep you from your loving heavenly Father.

I remember after one of our services, a young teenage girl, Kim, came up for prayer. She had a dark hardness about her, and her face was filled with anger. As we talked, she could barely look me in the eyes. She told me how she had been cutting and was experiencing demonic dreams almost every night. I asked her about her parents, and she quickly told me how much she hated her dad, who left years ago.

As I gently put my hand on her shoulder, she shuddered and pulled back. I waited a moment and then I asked the Father to come fill her heart with his love and reveal to her that she was his beloved daughter, in whom he was well pleased. As I prayed, I could feel his tangible love washing over her. The moment I said amen, she sprang forward, buried her tear-stained face in my chest, and wouldn't let go. The love of the Father was healing her heart.

The next week, she came forward again, but her appearance was so different that I didn't even recognize her. Someone had to tell me that it was Kim. She looked like a completely different person. Her eyes were soft and full of hope. Her face was bright and radiated beauty. Her words were brave and full of life. The Father's love had set her free.

That is the way of the Father. He says, "I have loved you with an everlasting love; I have drawn you with loving-kindness" (Jeremiah 31:3). Your Father says, *I see you! I want you! I believe you! I love you! I am proud of you! You are beautiful! You have what it takes!* "I will be a Father to you, and you will be my sons and daughters" (2 Corinthians 6:18). What God wants more than anything is to draw you into his family. Although he is a Healer, Provider, Forgiver, and Creator, he wants to be known as Father. He wants you to know him as Father because Father is not what he does; it is who he is. It's because he is a Father that he heals, provides, forgives, and creates. It is one thing to *know God is Father,* but it's entirely different to *experience him as Father.* Maybe it's time for a new experience.

THE FATHER'S EMBRACE

The most famous parable Jesus ever told has got to be the story of the prodigal son (see Luke 15:11–32). It's a story we resonate with because if we haven't been the prodigal, we have certainly been the older brother.

"I want my inheritance, and I want it now." In other words, *Dad, I wish you were dead.* The younger son in the parable thought freedom was found in independence, not in submission to his father. But life on our own is never as fun as we think it is.

The older brother, on the other hand, thought, "I'll earn my inheritance," meaning, *Dad, I'll make you proud of me.* He stayed home but never enjoyed his father, or life, because he was too busy performing in the fields. Both of the sons had orphaned hearts, so the father "divided his property between them" (Luke 15:12).

> Sometimes it takes the pig-pen to realize we have always had the palace.

Parties, prostitutes, and wild living quickly drained the younger son's fortune, until one day he woke up to realize he had blown his entire inheritance. He obviously never took Dave

Ramsey's Financial Peace class. After hitting rock bottom, he hired himself out to feed pigs. As he dreamed about feasting on pig slop, he started thinking about the abundance of his father's kingdom. You know you are in a mess when pig food starts to look appetizing. *Maybe I can go home and just be a hired hand. Anything would be better than this,* he thought. Sometimes it takes the pigpen to realize we have always had the palace. So he rehearsed a little apology speech and headed home, not because he was sorry but because he was hungry. But the prodigal son story is not about a boy's sins; it's about a father's love.

> "I will set out and go back to my father and say to him: Father, I have sinned against heaven and against you. I am no longer worthy to be called your son; make me like one of your hired men." So he got up and went to his father.
>
> But while he was still a long way off, his father saw him and was filled with compassion for him; he ran to his son, threw his arms around him and kissed him.
>
> The son said to him, "Father, I have sinned against heaven and against you. I am no longer worthy to be called your son."
>
> But the father said to his servants, "Quick! Bring the best robe and put it on him. Put a ring on his finger and sandals on his feet. Bring the fattened calf and kill it. Let's have a feast and celebrate. For this son of mine was dead and is alive again; he was lost and is found." (Luke 15:18–24)

Every day since the son left home, the father had been look-ing out over the horizon, hoping today would be the day. So when he saw his son walking home, he burst off the porch and ran to him. He grabbed his pig-smelling son and embraced him with a tender hug.

Even though we might walk to the Father, he always runs to us. It's his love that leads us to repentance, not our repentance that leads to his love. The Father always goes first.

"Father, I am no longer worthy to be called your son." That's honestly how many of us feel, isn't it? We know where we have been, what we have done, and the secrets that we keep. Our hearts say, *I am not worthy to be called your son or daughter, so let me work in your field and I'll earn my own way.* But the Father re-fused to empower the lie, so he interrupted him: "Give *my son* a robe, a ring, and sandals." A robe to cover his shame, a ring to establish his authority in the father's kingdom, and sandals as a reminder of his place as a son in the family. It was the father de-claring, "You are my beloved son in whom I am well pleased." The son's shame was covered, his authority was restored, his iden-tity was declared, and his fear was driven out. That deserves a party!

For the first time in his life, the son wasn't just alive; he was living. His father's embrace changed everything. Had his father not given him an embrace but instead had simply given him a robe, a ring, and sandals and walked back into the house, the son would have spent his life believing that he was no longer worthy to be a son. He would have slaved away in the fields, trying to earn his father's love and approval—trying to pay his father back. But because his father embraced him, he received the freedom of a father's love. His shame and his striving melted away in the arms of love. The love of his father changed the sign in his heart from "No Longer Worthy" to "Beloved Son."

We all need that kind of embrace.

Even Jesus received it. The freedom we see in Jesus's life didn't come from being immersed in the righteousness of God (himself), the waters of baptism, or even the Holy Spirit. He was free because he was immersed in the Father's love, as the word *beloved* was shouted from heaven the day of his baptism. You see, a lot of us have received the robe, the ring, and the sandals, but we have yet to receive the Father's love. We believe we are forgiven, Spirit empowered, and children of God, but we have never experienced (been immersed in) the Father's love for ourselves, so we still live like slaves. And until his healing love fills the cracks in our hearts, we will always perform for approval. Without the Father's embrace, we become like the older brother: home but never at rest, trying to earn a love that's already ours. It's only in receiving the Father's love that we are free to truly live.

The younger son thought life would be better without the cloud. The older brother performed for the cloud out of religious duty. Jesus, the perfect Son, followed the cloud because he knew the fullness of life was found with his good Father. How about you? Ultimately, your willingness to follow the cloud is based on your belief in the goodness of the Father. The underlying question we ask with each next step he invites us to take is "Can God be trusted?" And whatever sign is hanging in your heart determines your answer.

I don't know what your sign reads, but maybe it's time to trade it in for one that reads, "Beloved Son" or "Beloved Daughter."

Follow the Cloud—Live Free

Name five people you're trying to please right now.
What specific expectation are you trying to meet in
each of them? Is all that energy and effort getting you
the results you're hoping for? If not, what's it getting
you?

Look back at the list of characteristics of spiritual orphans and beloved sons and daughters. Which cat-
egory looks more like your life? Be honest. If you
answered "spiritual orphan," what is one characteris-
tic you'd like to see change first? Take a moment and
ask for that, pray *Father* . . .

EXPERIENCE HIS PRESENCE

YOU WERE NEVER MEANT TO BE ALONE

7

THUNDEROUS WHISPER

You saw how the LORD your God carried
you, as a father carries his son, all the way
you went until you reached this place.

—Deuteronomy 1:31

Y ou will fail."

Those were the words I heard at lunch as I asked some leaders I trusted and respected for counsel.

At that time, I had been the lead pastor of our church for less than two years. God was moving, the church was exponentially growing, and we were out of space. We were seeking God for wisdom on what to do next, and we were blown away by what we heard him say. We believed God asked us to follow the pattern of Acts 1:8: "You will receive power when the Holy Spirit comes on you; and you will be my witnesses in Jerusalem [your city], and in all Judea and Samaria [your region], and to the ends of the earth [the other side of the world]." We felt as if God was inviting us to take a next step in all three areas: to double the size of our current campus in our city, build a second campus in our region, and start a ministry school for church planters in India—all at the same time for fourteen million dollars.

Now, you have to understand, for the size of our church and the lack of experience we had as leaders at that time, this was literally an impossible vision. This was like Noah building the ark, the walls of Jericho coming down, or Peter walking on water. It was completely beyond our capacity in every way. Oh, and we believed that God was telling us not to do a fund-raising campaign but rather to simply cast the vision and invite people to be part of expanding God's kingdom.

Looking back on it, I understand why these experienced church leaders looked at me like I was crazy. "You will fail," they said. "There is no way you can do all of this. You will never raise that kind of money. You don't have the leadership experience. And you absolutely need to do a campaign fund-raiser and find consultants to help you." Passionately, they tried to talk me out of this "ridiculous idea." So I left the lunch meeting that day full of doubt. I questioned the vision, I questioned our team, I questioned myself, and I questioned God. *Did I really hear your voice?* But that is Satan's oldest trick. He tries to get us to question what God has said. Satan said to Eve in the Garden of Eden, "Did God really say, 'You must not eat from any tree in the garden'?" (Genesis 3:1). *Did God really say to change careers? Did God really say to marry this person? Did God really say I am loved? Did God really say to patiently wait?* He will use circumstances, people, and even our own emotions to make us question God's voice. But in my heart, I couldn't shake what I knew our leadership team had heard in unity from the Lord. So together we moved forward.

The day I got up to share this vision with our church, I was terrified. Ten minutes before the service, I was hiding like a little kid in a small room behind the platform. Those words kept echoing in my mind:

> The cloud always provides wherever he guides.

You will fail! And then all kinds of other voices started chiming in, saying, *This is crazy. What are we doing? This is impossible. I can't ask people for fourteen million dollars. We are too small. We don't have enough leaders. I wonder if we can get our deposit back?*

I had a choice to make: I had to decide whose voice I was going to follow. Was it going to be, "God said_____, so I_____," or, "They said_____, so I_____"? It's the same decision you and I have to make every day. We have to decide whose voice we will value. I didn't know how we were going to do it, but I knew what God had said. It was time for me to either follow by faith or flee in fear. So with a quivering voice and shaking hands, I walked onto the platform and shared the vision with our church. God's voice gave me the courage to follow the cloud into the impossible. And you know what? Our church overwhelmingly responded to the vision. Together we took our next step. And two and half years later, all three buildings of our next step were full of new people, and we were completely debt free. We didn't fail; we flourished, because the cloud always provides wherever he guides.

Words of Life

One of the questions that I get asked all the time is, "How do I hear God's voice?" It's a great question, because our desire to hear him speak is more important than our actual ability. And the good news is that God wants us to hear his voice more than we want to listen. Cloud followers have a hunger for his voice. In fact, one of the most dangerous heart postures we can have is as a follower of Jesus without a desire to hear his voice—to want what he offers without wanting him. Following him without listening to his voice is to choose religion over relationship. Sadly, that is the choice the Israelites made.

> When the people saw the thunder and lightning and heard
> the trumpet and saw the mountain in smoke, they
> trembled with fear. They stayed at a distance and said to
> Moses, "Speak to us yourself and we will listen. But do not
> have God speak to us or we will die."
> Moses said to the people, "Do not be afraid." (Exodus
> 20:18–20)

As the cloud drew near, they pulled away. Their hearts were still afraid of a God who had just put his love on display by setting them free. They were willing to follow God; they just weren't willing to hear his voice. They were willing to be the people of God; they just weren't willing to talk to him. So they said to Moses, "You go talk to God for us. You meet with God, hear what he has to say, and then come tell us what he said. We will listen to you, but we can't meet with God for ourselves!" They were afraid that if they heard his voice, they would die. But the truth is that we die without it. Jesus said, "The words I have spoken to you are spirit and they are life" (John 6:63). His voice is our life. Therefore, life without his voice is no life at all. The same voice that spoke the universe into existence, raised people from the dead, and calmed the wind and the waves wants to speak to us today. We don't die from the sound of his voice; we die without it.

But the Israelites preferred having Moses as a mediator rather than having a personal relationship with God. They wanted a real-estate agent to broker a deal for them instead of going on a date with someone who was already in love with them. And because they never listened to his voice, they never got to know his heart. The Israelites knew what God could do, but only Moses knew who God really was (see Psalm 103:7).

Think about my kids for a moment. Imagine if I provided for all their needs, drove them to school, fed them, and paid for everything in their lives but they never wanted to listen to me. Maybe you know what that is like. My kids and I would be related, but we wouldn't be in relationship. They would enjoy the work of my hands without getting to know the love of my heart. Sadly, I think that often describes our relationships with God.

I wonder how many of us are related to God but not in relationship with him. How often do we enjoy what he does without ever getting to know who he is? Jesus said, "Out of the overflow of the heart the mouth speaks" (Matthew 12:34). Put bluntly, whatever we say exposes who we really are. Our words are a reflection of our hearts. So God's voice reveals his heart. The more we hear his voice, the more we'll know his heart. And the more we know his heart, the more we'll trust his voice. To ignore his voice is to ignore God himself. We can't be in relationship with someone we never listen to.

SECONDHAND JESUS

Do you remember the telephone game from when you were a kid? Maybe you played it in school. One person whispers a phrase into someone's ear, and then he whispers it into the next person's ear. Each person passes it on to the next person until the message gets to the last person and she shouts the phrase out loud. What started as "Summer break is almost here" ends up as "Summer has been canceled this year." The further you got away from the source of the whisper, the more distorted the phrase became. The same is true with God. The further we get away from him as the source, the more distorted the truth becomes. And the more distorted the phrase becomes, the more costly the consequences are. God doesn't primarily want to speak to you through other people; he wants to speak directly to you. I wonder what truth is distorted in your life because you have heard it through the "telephone" of others instead of from the source.

Too often, like the Israelites, we drift into the danger zone. We want someone else to hear God for us—a pastor, a radio preacher, a friend, a spouse, or our grandma "who is very religious." But we were never meant to hear God's voice primarily through man. We were meant to hear God's voice from his mouth. Jesus died so we could have direct access to God. As a matter of fact, when someone else tells us what God has said, it usually still leaves us with doubt.

For example, what if Peter never heard Jesus's voice for himself? Imagine how different his life would have been. What if the Gospel account of Peter walking on water looked like this?

Jesus comes walking on the water toward the disciples' boat. After Jesus talks to the disciples for a few minutes, Peter leans over to John and asks, "What's Jesus saying?" John replies, "Um, he wants you to walk on water." Peter laughs. "What? Are you crazy? That's impossible. He didn't say that. Come on, man, what did he really say?" John glances at Jesus *and then turns back to Peter. "Yep, he wants you to walk out on the water to him. Go for it. We will be cheering you on from the boat."*

Secondhand Jesus will never give us firsthand faith.

There is no way that Peter would have gotten out of the boat if he hadn't heard Jesus for himself. And there is no way we will get out of our boats if we don't hear his voice for ourselves. To follow the cloud is to hear his voice. If faith comes by hearing, then our willingness to listen is what gives us the faith to follow (see Romans 10:17). But if we are always waiting for other people to tell us what God has said, our hearts will always be full of doubt: *Did God really say that?* This is why so many of us struggle with following the cloud. Secondhand Jesus will never give us firsthand faith. We can't follow the cloud through the voice of man, but one word from God can change everything.

Tune In

As my kids have grown, it has changed the conversations we have together. Regardless of their ages, I have always spoken to them on their levels. When they were babies, I goo-gooed and gaa-gaaed. When they started crawling, I used that high-pitched, "Look at how big you are" voice. When they began school, I started using bigger words to communicate to them.

> The real question isn't, *Is God speaking?* It's, *Are we listening?*

Now as they are learning to read, we are having grown-up conversations. As a dad, I have always spoken to them in a way they could understand. I have never demanded my kids to converse with me on my level; I have always adjusted my words to match their levels of understanding. The same is true with God. He isn't speaking to us in a cryptic code, a foreign language, or in King James English. God doesn't use big theological terms, churchy words, or phrases that need an interpreter. He doesn't sound like an old-time angry preacher. He speaks to us on our level in ways we understand. He is a good Father who uses the universal language of love.

Jesus wants us to confidently believe that we can hear his voice. He said, "Man does not live on bread alone, but on every word that comes from the mouth of God" (Matthew 4:4). The word *comes* is present tense and means that God hasn't spoken to us just in the past but that he is constantly speaking to us now. So

God is continually speaking to us, "and his sheep follow him because they know his voice" (John 10:4). Are you one of Jesus's sheep? Is Jesus your shepherd? If yes, then he says you know how to hear his voice.

Let me illustrate it for you like this. When you were born on this earth, you were born with the innate ability to hear in the physical realm. You didn't have to grow ears. You didn't have to figure out how to hear. You were born with the ability to hear the sounds of the world. You just had to learn to tune in to your father's voice and learn the language he was speaking. You had to learn to ignore the clutter of the clicks, pops, booms, bangs, screams, and yells to tune in to the voice of the one holding you.

Jesus says that when you, by faith, believe in him, you are born again. And when you are born again, you are born with the innate ability to hear in the spiritual realm. You are born again with spiritual ears and have the ability to hear God's voice. You have the ability to hear the sounds of heaven. You just have to learn to tune into his voice and learn the language he is speaking. You have to learn to ignore the distractions of shame, condemnation, criticism, doubt, negativity, and busyness and tune in to the voice of the one holding you.

Beloved sons and daughters hear the voice of their Father. "Whether you turn to the right or to the left, *your ears will hear a voice* behind you, saying, 'This is the way; walk in it'" (Isaiah 30:21). The real question isn't, *Is God speaking?* It's, *Are we listening?*

Value His Voice

A few years ago, I set up a meeting with a well-known leader in our region. It took months to finally get an appointment, but because I love to learn, I was willing to wait as long as it took. The day of our lunch, I drove an hour to get to the restaurant. I arrived twenty minutes early with specific questions written in my notebook that I wanted to ask him. When he walked into the restaurant, I introduced myself, and the first thing he said to me was, "How did you get on my calendar?"

I was completely taken aback and didn't know how to respond. Again, in a frustrated tone, he said, "How did you get on my calendar? I don't have time for this. You have fifteen minutes to talk about whatever you want."

We sat down, and for the next fifteen minutes, he looked at his phone the entire time I tried to talk with him. Eventually, I just stopped asking questions, and he didn't even realize it. I paid for our meal, easily one of the most awkward lunches of my life.

As I drove home, I wondered how often I do that to God.

We say we want to hear him speak, but sometimes our actions communicate otherwise. Our lifestyle often says, *God, how did you get on my calendar? I don't have time for this. Just say what you want to say, because I gotta go.* God is speaking, but we aren't always listening. If we want to hear his voice, we need to position ourselves in a posture to listen. Like Samuel, a little boy who learned how to hear God's voice, the cry of our hearts must be "Speak, for your servant is listening" (1 Samuel 3:10). You can't start following the cloud until you are first willing to listen.

So how can we position ourselves to hear what God is saying?

Slow down. Our lives are insanely busy. We fill our days so full of activities, sports, commitments, gatherings, and travel that there is no room left for God. Our phones have become permanently attached to us, allowing the voices of the world to have instant access to us wherever we go. The TV, iTunes, and Internet are constantly filling our ears with noise. I'm just saying if we have more interaction with our technology than we do with the Holy Spirit, something is wrong. And while we are running around through life, we expect God to speak to us in the midst of all these other voices. But God won't compete for our attention. He wants us to slow down and listen—to come to him with quiet anticipation and value his voice above all others.

In fact, why don't you put this book down, turn off your electronics, sit quietly for a few minutes, and just listen. Can you do that without getting antsy? We say, "God, I can't hear you. Speak louder." God says, *Be still and listen.* We want God to turn his voice up; he wants us to turn our lives down.

Engage the Scriptures. God writes like he speaks. His voice sounds like his word. Therefore, his written word teaches us how to hear his spoken word. Put differently, what God has already said will prepare you to hear what he wants to say. If "all Scripture is God-breathed" (2 Timothy 3:16), then the Bible reveals to us what God's voice sounds like. Actually, if you want to hear him speak right now, open your Bible. Those are the words he has already said, and a word of God once spoken continues to be spoken. Whatever value you give to the written word is the value you have already assigned to his spoken word (see John 5:47). People who read his Word hear his voice.

Seek him. To demand that God speak violates the relationship. You can't demand people to speak, but you can prepare yourself to listen. For example, if I try to force my wife, Colleen, to talk to me, it usually doesn't go all that well. But when I stop what I am doing, go out of my way to find her, and look her in the eyes, she will share her heart with me. The same is true with God. He is waiting for us to prepare our hearts to listen. Moses turned to the side and went to see the burning bush. Jesus often withdrew to lonely places to pray. David stepped out of the chaos to inquire of the Lord. And they heard God speak. When we change what we are doing and look for God, we will hear him speak.

Pursue godly relationships. One of the greatest ways we learn how to hear God's voice is by getting around other people who know how to listen to him. If you are serious about hearing God, then you need a small group of people who will help you tune in to his voice. I love being around people who hear God because it always builds my faith. Hearing about what God has been saying to them helps me hear what he wants to say to me.

Joshua learned how to hear God from Moses. Timothy learned how to listen to the Holy Spirit from Paul. The disciples learned to tune in to the Father from Jesus. People who know what God's voice sounds like will help you discern his voice in your own life. Positioning yourself in godly relationships in which you talk about, learn about, and become more like Jesus together is a key to hearing the voice of God. Proverbs 13:20 tells us that you will become like whomever you are walking with. Faith is contagious, while doubt is infectious. When you are around people who believe that God speaks, your faith will rise, but when you are around people who are full of unbelief, their doubt will infect your heart. Are you walking with the right people?

Ask for confirmation. Whenever you believe you have heard God speak, it's a good idea to seek confirmation. In a world full of voices competing for our attention, it's not only okay but also wise to ask, "God, was that really you?" And you can answer that question by simply running what you believe you have heard through these filters:

- Does it align with Scripture?
- Does godly counsel confirm it?
- Is there a sacred echo? (Am I hearing it in more than one place/from more than one person?)
- Does it require faith?
- Does it lead you toward Jesus?

Remember, God's voice is always loving, will give you peace, and bring you comfort. If it doesn't pass through these filters, it wasn't God. If it does, you can move forward with confidence.

ASK, LISTEN, RESPOND

At Valley Creek, we define ourselves as a Jesus-focused, Spirit-filled, life-giving church. We believe that Jesus-focused people focus more on what Jesus has done for them than on what they have to do for him, Spirit-filled people walk in the character and power of Jesus, and life-giving people receive and release the life of God wherever they go.

Our vision is *to help people take the next step on their journey with Jesus.* It's an inspiring vision because its simplicity makes it relevant to everyone. No matter how long we have walked with God, we always have a next step. Whether it's to come back to church next weekend, forgive someone, start serving, or grow as a leader, we all have a next step, and only God can tell us what it is. What I love about our vision is that it invites every individual to hear God for themselves.

> *Ask* God what he wants to say. *Listen* to his voice. *Respond* with obedience by taking your next step.

I don't know what your next step is, so I can't tell you what to do. But God knows. "The Lord says, 'I will guide you along the best pathway for your life. I will advise you and watch over you'" (Psalm 32:8, NLT). So we use this little phrase: *Ask, Listen, and Respond. Ask* God what he wants to say. *Listen* to his voice. *Respond* with obedience by taking your next step. The heart of a cloud follower is "I asked ___. He said ___. Therefore, I will ___!"

Only God's voice gives us the clarity and courage to move forward. Moses confronted Pharaoh, Paul became a church planter, and Jesus went to the cross because God's voice gave them the faith to walk into the unknown. God will ask you to take next steps that are beyond your ability and understanding, but his voice will bring you the peace and confidence to get up and go.

Even as I am writing this, our church is about to take another huge next step. As I look at the obstacles and challenges in front of us, it feels impossible. The voices of the world are telling me to

pull away, but I know what God has said. And if all God's promises are a "Yes" in Jesus, then we not only can but we must move
forward, trusting his voice. It's only in the impossible where we
discover the God of possibility. If he has said it, he will complete
it. We just need to have the faith to follow.

LEANING IN

I don't know about you, but sometimes I wish God would speak
to me in the spectacular. I would love for him to write a message
in the sky, give me a burning bush, send me an angel, speak with
a booming voice from heaven, or talk to me through a donkey
(okay, how about at least through a dog or cat?). I mean, how cool
would it be to get a text message from God? *Buzz. Buzz.* You pull
out your phone. It's an unknown number. You open the text message and it reads, "Hey, it's God. The answer to your question is
yes!" Although that would be awesome, and so much easier, we
have something even better: the Holy Spirit.

The Holy Spirit inside of you is better than Jesus next to you.
That's why Jesus told
the disciples it was
good for him to leave
because then the Holy
Spirit could come.
Jesus died so that any-

> The unending presence
> of God gives us the faith
> to hear the unfailing
> voice of God.

one could hear the voice of God anytime, anywhere. Jesus said,
"When he, the Spirit of truth, comes, he will guide you into all
truth. He will not speak on his own; he will speak only what he

hears, and he will tell you what is yet to come" (John 16:13). The Holy Spirit is your built-in navigation system and he never says, "Recalculating." We don't need a formal road map, because we have a personal tour guide. He is our Counselor, who speaks the wisdom of God to our hearts. The unending presence of God gives us the faith to hear the unfailing voice of God. He is the great Whisperer within us, and that *is spectacular.*

Do you remember the prophet Elijah? In 1 Kings 19, he was having one of the worst days of his life. There are a lot of worst days in the Bible. That should bring you a little comfort. Even the best of us have bad days. Elijah was discouraged, he had a minis-

> We want his voice to be in the spectacular so we don't miss *it,* but God wants his voice to be in a whisper so we don't miss *him.*

try hangover, he was exhausted, and he was running from a crazy woman who wanted to kill him. While he was resting in a cave, God came to meet with him.

Now here is where it gets interesting. A great wind ripped down the mountain and broke open the rocks—but God was not in the wind. Then a giant earthquake shook the foundation of the mountain—but God was not in the earthquake. Then a fire burned everything on the side of the mountain—but God was not in the fire. Then came a gentle whisper—and God was in the whisper. So Elijah pulled his cloak over his face, leaned into the presence of God, and listened. The power of heaven wasn't in the spectacular; it was in the whisper.

You might wonder, *Why does God most often speak in a whisper?* He whispers because he is close and desires to be closer still. God is not somewhere way off in the universe. He is right here, and his whisper is our invitation to lean into him. It's an invitation to intimacy. The intent of the voice of God is always to draw us closer to the heart of God. We want his voice to be in the spectacular so we don't miss *it,* but God wants his voice to be in a whisper so we don't miss *him.*

Follow the Cloud—Live Free

God wants you to hear his voice even more than you want to listen. When is the last time you felt as though you clearly heard God speak to you? What was going on in your life? Take a moment, quiet yourself down, and *Ask, Listen,* and *Respond* about an area of life where you need God's wisdom. He promises he will give it to you (James 1:5).

If we want to hear God speak, we have to position ourselves to listen. Which of the areas of valuing his voice are the easiest for you? Which are the most challenging? Slowing down? Engaging the Scriptures? Seeking him? Pursuing godly relationships? Or asking for confirmation? Why are they the most challenging?

8

FINDING FRIENDSHIP

wonder what that conversation would have been like.

Abraham must have rehearsed it in his mind at least a thousand times. "Um, Sarah, did you do something new with your hair? Because, wow, it looks amazing—I love it. I was thinking maybe we could have your mom over for dinner next week. Hey, uhhhh, you know our son, Isaac? Yeah, the one we waited more than twenty-five years for? Well [*gulp*], God asked me to offer him as a sacrifice on the mountain. I know it sounds crazy, and I know you are going to say no, but before you say anything, I believe that God will bring him back from the dead. So if it's okay with you, we are going to head out first thing in the morning and see what happens."

On second thought, maybe he just told her he was going to take Isaac for a walk.

"'Abraham!'

'Here I am,' [Abraham] replied.

Then God said, 'Take your son, your only son, Isaac, whom you love, and go to the region of Moriah. Sacrifice him there as a burnt offering on one of the mountains I will tell you about'" (Genesis 22:1–2). Some steps are harder than others. Sometimes our desire to hear God speak can quickly be replaced by our desire for him to be silent. I am sure that in this moment, Abraham wished he could have ignored the voice of God. But once we hear him speak, we are responsible to steward what he has said, regardless of the cost.

> Whatever you do with what God said yesterday will determine what you will hear tomorrow.

Stewardship has always been a big deal to God. He wants us to be good stewards of everything he has entrusted to us: finances, relationships, opportunities, talents, anointing, ministries, and especially his voice. If we are faithful with little, he promises he will entrust us with much. Jesus said, "Consider carefully what you hear. . . . With the measure you use, it will be measured to you—and even more. Whoever has will be given more; whoever does not have, even what he has will be taken from him" (Mark 4:24–25). In other words, whatever you do with what God said yesterday will determine what you will hear tomorrow. Our ability to hear what God wants to say is determined by what we have done with what God has already said. God isn't careless with his words. They contain so much life and so much power that he entrusts them to those who will use them wisely. Obedience is how we steward God's voice.

RUN THE PLAY

Think about your favorite football team for a moment. Let's say it's the championship game and everything is on the line. The team huddles together and the coach calls in a strategic play for them to run. Each player has a unique assignment based on the play that is called. The players confidently break the huddle and head to the line of scrimmage, knowing exactly what they are supposed to do. As they line up, the center puts his hand on the ball, the defense is ready, and the crowd is holding its breath. But imagine if instead of running the play, they turned around, high-fived each other, and headed back to the huddle to get another play. That would be ridiculous. There is no reason to huddle again, because they already know the play they are supposed to run. The coach isn't going to call in another play until they run the one that he has already given them. The same is true with God.

When we hear God speak, it's our responsibility to combine his voice with our faith and simply run the play he gives us. To resist his commands is to resist God himself. I believe we hear God speak; we just aren't sure we want to obey. We don't want God to talk to us about tithing, serving, or forgiving; we want him to talk to us about blessing, abundance, and the answers to our prayers.

You won't always like the play that is called. You won't always like what you hear God say. But to be in a relationship means you are willing to listen to what the other person wants to say, not just what you want to hear. Obedience tells God you're ready for more. So if you feel like you aren't hearing God's voice, go back and do the last thing he asked you to do.

Jesus said, "Blessed rather are those *who hear* the word of God *and obey* it" (Luke 11:28). We aren't blessed when we hear God speak. We are blessed when we apply what he has said to our lives—when we run the play he has called. Faith chooses to obey before God speaks because faith values relationship over comfort. And that's what Abraham did. He declared, "Here I am," long before God ever called because he had the heart of a true friend.

REASONABLE REQUESTS

I grew up outside of Buffalo, NY. Although Buffalo is known for its chicken wings and for losing the Super Bowl four times in a row (heartbreaking), it's probably most famous for its endless supply of snow. If you live anywhere near places like Buffalo, you quickly learn that you have one of two choices: constantly complain about the weather, or learn to embrace the snow. I chose to embrace it and tried to make a little money at the same time, so toward the end of college I started a snowplowing business.

I remember one time, around 3:00 a.m., the snow was falling a few inches an hour and I was plowing away. But as I carelessly pushed a big load of snow off the edge of the road, the worst thing that can happen to a snowplower happened to me: my truck got buried in a snowbank.

What do you do when you're stuck and it's 3:00 a.m., freezing cold, and snowing like crazy? You pretty much have one option—call someone to pull you out. As I scrolled through my phone, I saw the names of lots of people I knew. But what I needed in that moment was a friend—someone whose heart had already said, "I'm on my way," before I even called. Only relationship can get you out of a warm bed on a cold night. So I dialed a number, and ten minutes later I was back on the road drinking a fresh cup of coffee. That's friendship. Friends respond before the request is made because they believe the relationship outweighs the cost.

That's what made Abraham so special. When God called, he answered.

"Early the next morning Abraham got up. . . . He set out for the place God had told him about" (Genesis 22:3). That statement amazes me. I think we can all agree that this was not a reasonable request. Isaac was their miracle child and the fulfillment of God's promise. To sacrifice him was crazy. But Abraham took his next step without delay or hesitation. Abraham was so desperate for God that nothing was going to hold him back from following the cloud. He knew God loved him fiercely, so he held on to Isaac loosely and obeyed fully. Abraham understood what we often forget: obedience is determined by relationship, not reason.

The Bible is full of examples of God asking people to do things that didn't seem reasonable at the time. It wasn't reasonable for him to ask Noah to build a boat in the desert with no rain in the forecast. It wasn't reasonable for Nehemiah, a simple servant, to lead a nation to rebuild the walls of Jerusalem. It wasn't reasonable for David to fight Goliath with just a slingshot. And it's probably not *reasonable* for God to ask you to take your next step. Maybe he is asking you to humble yourself, move away from family, end

> Disobedience is simply misplaced trust. It's trusting in someone or something more than we trust in God.

a relationship, quit your team, start something new, change majors, or join a small group. And you think it's unreasonable for him to ask you to do that. You're right; it is. But obedience isn't determined by reason but by relationship.

We have to remember that we are called to walk by faith, not by sight, which means reason is the enemy of faith. Every step we are afraid to take is a place where we question the goodness of God. Disobedience is simply misplaced trust. It's trusting in someone or something more than we trust in God. We say no to God because we believe that saying yes to something else will make us happy. But if God is love, then every step he asks us to take is loving—every step, especially the ones that seem unreasonable. And if that is true, the *most reasonable* thing you will ever do is take every step he gives you.

> You are as close to God as you want to be.

A radical request is simply an invitation to experience a radical relationship.

"Was not our ancestor Abraham considered righteous for what he did when he offered his son Isaac on the altar? You see that his faith and his actions were working together. . . . And the scripture was fulfilled that says, 'Abraham believed God, and it was credited to him as righteousness,' *and he was called God's friend*" (James 2:21–23). God gave Abraham a radical request, and because Abraham *got up* and *set out,* he became a friend of God. Heaven records Abraham as God's friend because he said, "Here I am," not, "I can't do that." Cloud followers become God's friends because they say yes when he calls.

How Close Are You?

When it all comes down to it, you are as close to God as you want to be. In Jesus, you have full access to boldly approach the throne of grace (see Hebrews 4:16). The reason Moses, David, and Paul experienced God in ways no one else did was because they were willing to take the steps no one else would. God says, "You will seek me and find me when you seek me with all your heart" (Jeremiah 29:13). God is not found in casual exploration but in passionate pursuit. If you will obey him like no one else does, you will have a relationship with him like no one else does. The more of ourselves we surrender, the more of him we will encounter. Every next step takes you deeper into his heart.

> Jesus's obedience determines your identity, but your obedience determines your intimacy.

It's easy to think the "heroes of the faith" had a different access to God than we do. But you can be as close to God as anyone who has ever lived. Jesus said, "You are my friends *if* you do what I command" (John 15:14). In other words, obedience is the pathway to friendship with God.

Think about it like this: Jesus's obedience determines your identity, but your obedience determines your intimacy. Your willingness to obey doesn't affect your salvation, but it does influence the quality of your relationship. In other words, salvation is free, but obedience is the cost of deep friendship. To obey, you might have to give up that salary, hobby, comfort, convenience, routine, or whatever else you hold most dear. But as you become his friend, you start to realize it wasn't really a cost, because with him you always receive more than you give.

Imagine if I never did anything my wife, Colleen, asked me to do. What if I never did the dishes? What if I never took her out on dates? What if I never went walking with her? What if I never honored any requests she had? And what if I refused to change things she didn't like? If I never did anything she asked me to do, we would still be married, but our level of intimacy would be very low. My identity wouldn't change. I would still be her husband, we would still be in covenant, but we wouldn't *really* be friends. Our relationship would be superficial at best. You probably know a few marriages that look like that. Well, the same is true with God.

> Obedience is God's love language.

When we don't obey his commands, it doesn't change our identity. We are still beloved sons and daughters in covenant with him, but we don't move into deep friendship with him. To refuse our next step is to deny his friend request. Our disobedience doesn't change who we are, but it does determine the quality of our relationships. "Whoever has my commands and obeys them, he is the one who loves me" (John 14:21). In essence, obedience is God's love language. It's how he asks us to love him. Every next step we take declares, *God, I love you.*

Fear, Duty, or Love

If you have kids, then you probably know a noisy house is a healthy house. At least it is for us. As long as our home sounds like a circus, I am confident that everything is okay. If someone is crying about something, singing a made-up song, laughing uncontrollably, making obnoxious sounds, or crashing things, I know all is well. But quiet usually means trouble. So one afternoon when I hadn't heard any noise from my daughter in a while, I knew she was up to something.

Slowly, I crept up the stairs and peeked into her bedroom, and there she was, drawing a gigantic picture on the walls with lipstick!

As I watched little Miss Picasso working on her masterpiece, I wondered what Dr. Phil would do. Quietly, I backed away from her door and went to the top of the stairs. I was curious to see how she would respond, so I made a bunch of noise to let her know I was coming and said, "Hey, Emma, where are you?"

As I walked into her room, she instantly took the tube of lipstick and nervously started applying it to her lips.

"Hey, Emma, whatcha doing?"

"Nothing, Daddy. Just putting lipstick on. Don't I look so pretty?" she said.

"You look beautiful, but is that *really* what you are doing?" I asked.

"Yeah, Daddy. Just putting my makeup on. You want a kiss?" she anxiously said.

"Emma, are you telling me the truth?"

As big crocodile tears started to fall, she cried, "Noooooooooo. I am drawing a picture . . . on the wall . . . with lipstick."

"What have we said about that?" I asked.

Hesitantly, she replied, "That I can only draw on paper."

"So what does this mean?" I asked.

"That there has to be con-sha-quences," she said.

I replied, "Yeah, there has to be consequences. So I am going to take away your doll, Isabelle, for one week."

She was devastated. "Please don't take my dolly. Anything but my dolly," she begged.

"I'm sorry, Emma, but that is the con-sha-quence." So I put her doll downstairs in my office and tried to clean up the lipstick.

The next day I kept thinking about the situation. For months we had struggled with her drawing on the walls, floors, furniture— pretty much on everything except paper. Obviously, our parenting strategy wasn't working, so I wanted to try something different.

When I got home from work, I called her into my office. She walked in, still heartbroken over losing her doll, and could barely look me in the eyes. I reached up on the shelf, grabbed her doll, and said, "Here is your dolly."

Stunned, she said, "I can have her back? Why?"

"Because I love you and I forgive you." She hugged her doll and started to walk out of my office. When she got to the door, she stopped. What happened next shocked me. She dropped her doll on the ground, turned around, ran and jumped into my lap, gave me a huge hug, and said, "I love you, Daddy." She skipped out of my office, and you know what? She has never drawn on the walls again. Seriously. Why didn't I try that tactic the first time?

As I sat there speechless, I started to realize that is the power of grace. Although she expected con-sha-quences, it was undeserved kindness that transformed her heart. As simple as it may seem, one moment of grace not only changed her behavior but, more importantly, drew her into my arms. And that's what God's grace does for us.

Too often, we try to obey God out of fear or duty. We follow the cloud because we are afraid of consequences. We follow because we think we have to. But God wants us to follow out of our love for him, so he gives us grace—a grace that draws us into his arms and changes our behavior.

We often forget that when God gave the Israelites the Ten Commandments, the first sentence was a reminder of his grace in their lives: "I am the LORD your God, who brought you out of Egypt, out of the land of slavery" (Exodus 20:2). Before he asked them to follow, he reminded them that he had already set them free. Obedience is the natural response to receiving grace. Jesus knows that he who has been forgiven much loves much (Luke 7:47). Basically, when we understand *what he has done,* it will change *what we do.* Only grace can give us the *desire* and the *power* to obey out of love. The more grace I receive, the more I desire to obey. "[Grace] teaches us to say 'No' to ungodliness and worldly passions, and to live self-controlled, upright and godly lives" (Titus 2:12). Grace is our teacher. It doesn't empower us to sin; it empowers us to overcome sin. Genuine obedience starts by receiving God's grace.

In fact, his grace is so powerful that it empowers us to live beyond what the Law demands. The Law can tell us not to commit adultery, but only grace can give us the hearts to love our spouses. The Law can tell us not to steal, but only grace can give us the desire to be generous. The Law can tell us not to covet, but only grace can help us be grateful for our lives. The Law can tell us to follow out of fear or duty, but only grace can empower us to follow out of love.

Whenever we aren't willing to obey, it's because we have forgotten how much we have been forgiven. When we don't want to follow where the cloud is going, it's because we have lost sight of where we have been.

I Won't Go Without You

I don't know about you, but I am not very good at waiting. I don't like to wait in line, in traffic, at the DMV, or for the Internet to load. I admit it, I am impatient. Let's get on with it already.

So when I find myself waiting on Colleen to go on a date, I get a little crazy. Somehow it seems as if every time we go out, I end up waiting in the car while she is still getting ready. She has to do her makeup, put on her jewelry, change her outfit, and double-check on the kids, all while I am ready and waiting. "Honey, if we don't leave now, we are going to miss our reservation." I could leave and just go to dinner without her, but that would kind of defeat the purpose. Or when she is ready, I could pout and say, "Never mind. I don't want to go anymore. I'm busy doing something else now." But the point of our date isn't about getting to the restaurant on time; it's about being together. Enjoying each other is more important than getting wherever we wanted to go. The relationship is superior to the destination. The same is true with God.

One of the challenges of following the cloud is that God's timing is very different from ours. With him, a day is like a thousand years, and a thousand years is like a day. So the temptation we constantly face is to move when it's time to wait, and wait when it's time to move. "Whenever the cloud lifted from above the Tent, the Israelites set out; wherever the cloud settled, the Israelites encamped. . . . Whether the cloud stayed over the tabernacle for two days or a month or a year, the Israelites would remain in camp and not set out; but when it lifted, they would set out. At the LORD's command they encamped, and at the LORD's command they set out" (Numbers 9:17, 22–23).

God's desire was that his presence would always be at the center of their lives. The Israelites weren't meant to get ahead of (nor lag behind) the cloud, because it was their source of life. In fact, whenever they moved beyond the cloud, they always found themselves in trouble. That's why every night the entire nation would camp around the cloud. The point of following the cloud was never about *getting somewhere;* it was always about *enjoying someone.* Each step had less to do with getting to their destination and more to do with getting to know their God. It didn't matter if they had to wait or hurry; what mattered was that they were experiencing God. That's why Moses boldly declared, "If your Presence does not go with us, do not send us up from here" (Exodus 33:15). He refused to go anywhere without God. Moses believed that the desert with God was better than the Promised Land without God. He didn't care where he was or where he was going as long as he knew who he was with.

Obedience is choosing to say, *I would rather be here with you than go there by myself.* It's simply staying in step with God because we value the relationship more than the destination. Whenever we get out of alignment with the cloud, it's because we are more focused on getting somewhere than enjoying someone. We often want to get to that new job, relationship, or opportunity, or just get out of this current season so bad that we are willing to go without him. Without realizing it, we can become more interested in what God can do for us than we are in God himself. And when we don't feel that he is doing it for us, we tend to do it for ourselves.

But you don't want more than God's will for your life.

As a pastor, I watch people move on their own all the time: the guy who uproots his family to chase a few more bucks, the woman who continually quits relationships because she is afraid of vulnerability, the family who changes churches because of preference or offense, the person who wants to do a good thing at the wrong time. But just because we can do something doesn't mean we should. I am amazed by how often people make major decisions without ever asking God what he thinks. Maybe you have been there. I know I have.

Here's the question we have to ask ourselves: *Is God inviting me to follow, or am I just deciding to go?* Remember that everything you are looking for is found only where he is. "Better is one day in your courts than a thousand elsewhere; I would rather be a doorkeeper in the house of my God than dwell in the tents of the wicked" (Psalm 84:10). The psalmist reminds us that being a servant in the presence of God is better than being a king alone in this world. The heart of a cloud follower says, "I won't go without you."

ONE THING

Before I became the lead pastor, I served at Valley Creek for five years as an associate pastor. During that time, all I could think about was planting a church. I wanted to go back up north and start a new church. I had a great name picked out. I knew what our vision and ministry philosophy would be. I had dreams about what it was going to be like. I even had people willing to fund it. I was ready to go. So when our lead pastor pulled me into his office and asked me to make a long-term commitment and take the associate pastor role, my initial response was, "I'm sorry but I can't. I am going to go plant a church." Well, I didn't say that, but I certainly thought it. What I said was, "Let me pray about it."

Over the next few days, I prayed and was fully expecting that God was going to agree with my great plan to plant a church. But instead I clearly heard the Lord say, *Johnny, I can do more in two days than you can do in two years. Will you serve me by serving your pastor?* I couldn't believe it. Instead of telling me to go, he was asking me to stay. I felt as if God was saying that I could go ahead without him and struggle for two years trying to start a church, or patiently wait for his timing. Sometimes your next step is to wait. And as hard as it is, waiting on God is never wasted time.

So I stayed when everything in me wanted to go. I stayed not because I wanted to but because God asked me to. For the next two years, the cloud didn't move. And looking back, that was the greatest thing that could have happened to me. In my desperation to go, I learned to be aware of God in the now. During that season, I discovered that he wasn't just *for me* but that he was *with me*.

> Sometimes your next step is to wait. And as hard as it is, waiting on God is never wasted time.

Then one day, as suddenly as it had stopped, the cloud moved. Our pastor was sent to China as a missionary, and almost two years to the day I heard God speak, I became the lead pastor of Valley Creek Church. As I stood up to preach to more than a thousand people that first weekend, I remembered what the Lord had said. In one weekend—two days—he gave me more than I could have built in two years by myself. And instead of planting one church, I am now leading a church that is planting churches around the world.

What I have learned is that following the cloud is always the fastest way to get where you are going. God can do more in two days than you can do in two years. Even though it often feels as if he is taking you the long way around, his detour is faster than your freeway. If Jesus is Lord, then you give up the right to determine the direction of your life. The cloud will go left when you want it to go right. It will speed up when you want it to slow down. And it will stop when you are desperate for it to go. The only thing predictable about the cloud is that it is unpredictable. But life is not about doing something or going somewhere; it's about being *with* someone, and his name is Jesus.

> Sometimes it's harder to trust God when he says *wait* than it is to trust him when he says *go.*

We often talk about these huge adventurous steps of faith, such as defeating giants, killing lions, and conquering cities (changing careers, launching new ministries, and moving somewhere we have never been). But sometimes the smallest steps are the hardest ones. Being kind to a stranger, reading your Bible, saying *I'm sorry,* choosing joy, and being grateful can be the most difficult steps because we don't see the significance in them. In reality, waiting often takes more courage than going. Sometimes it's harder to trust God when he says *wait* than it is to trust him when he says *go.* It's in those moments that we have to remind ourselves that life is not about getting somewhere; it's about enjoying someone. If we don't enjoy God where we are, we won't enjoy him where we are going.

Every step, whether in the waiting or the going, is designed to keep us desperately dependent upon the one thing that matters: him! "One thing I ask of the LORD, this is what I seek: that I may dwell in the house of the LORD all the days of my life, to gaze upon the beauty of the LORD" (Psalm 27:4). Cloud followers want one thing: friendship with God. So like Abraham, they boldly say, "Here I am," long before God ever calls.

Follow the Cloud—Live Free

Stewardship is a big deal to God. You might be good at stewarding your finances, talents, and relationships, but how well do you steward God's voice? Said another way, how have you responded to what God has said to you in the past? What is the last play God called in your life—the last thing he asked you to do? Have you fully run that play? If not, who or what is holding you back?

9

LIVING IN SECURITY

I have a famous right shoulder. Let me explain.

I love to learn. I am always looking for opportunities to grow and develop as a leader. I'm a big believer that it is our responsibility to fan into flame the gifts that have been given to us. So when I was invited through a friend of a friend to participate in a round-table discussion with fifteen high-profile leaders, I was thrilled. I am not sure how or why I got invited, but I was grateful for the opportunity.

The day of the discussion, I nervously introduced myself to each leader. I felt like I was out of my league and wondered what I would be able to contribute to the conversation. For the next few hours, I listened as a variety of topics were batted around. At the end of the night, we snapped a group picture, I had taken five pages of notes in my journal, and I left full of faith. It was a great day.

A few weeks later, after one of our weekend services, I was unwinding on the couch watching football. Scrolling through Twitter, I saw that one of the guys had posted the group picture from the roundtable. As I opened it up, I couldn't believe what I saw. They had cropped me out of the picture.

Seriously.

All you could see was the edge of my right shoulder. Fourteen guys and my right shoulder.

I kept looking at my phone thinking, *Are you kidding me? You cropped me out of the picture? Who* does *that?* Everything in me wanted to reply and post the picture that had everyone in it with a caption that said, "Hey, here is my other shoulder." But no one ever wins when you emotionally respond on social media.

> Insecurity is chronic self-consciousness.

As I sat there with hurt feelings, I wondered, *Why did they crop me out? What's wrong with me? I guess I'm not a good-enough leader. Maybe I'm not cool enough to be their friend. Maybe I really don't belong.* Feelings of inadequacy and rejection flooded my heart. I started to question my relational skills, my leadership ability, and even my calling as a pastor. It's amazing how something so small can make you question so much. As I was having my own pity party, I felt the Lord ask me, *Why do you care so much about what they think? Why are you letting them make you question what I have called you to do?* In that moment, my insecurities were exposed and the Lord was inviting me to confront them.

I would guess that at some point you have been there too. Maybe you weren't cropped out of a picture, but you have probably experienced feelings of rejection, inadequacy, and inferiority. Moments where your insecurities were exposed. Moments that made you question who you are and who you aren't.

> We weren't meant to live *with insecurity;* we were meant to live *in security.*

Let's face it: Insecurity is exhausting. It makes us compare ourselves to others, doubt our abilities, question our worth, and overemphasize our weaknesses. Insecurity is chronic self-consciousness. It's the constant evaluation and judgment of self. The insecure mind is full of "I should be more ___" or "I am not enough of ___" or "I wish I were like ___" or "I can't ___." You can probably fill in those blanks pretty easily. I know I can. We are really good at focusing on our failures and flaws, and the world is really good at pointing them out. It's easy to compare what's wrong with us to what's right with everyone else. But we weren't meant to live *with insecurity;* we were meant to live *in security.* Actually, every insecurity in our lives is a bondage God wants to break. And even though it may be uncomfortable for us, he will expose our insecurities so that he can make us secure in him.

WHO AM I?

It's hard to read the Bible without coming to the conclusion that God loves the underdog. He loves to choose the most unlikely people (the most insecure people) to accomplish his purposes. The last people we would pick are usually the first ones he empowers. Jacob was a deceiver, Rahab was a prostitute, Matthew was a tax collector, and Mary was a teenager. That's good news for us because it means we are positioned to be chosen by God for great things. Our weakness qualifies us for God's strength.

When God chose Moses the murderer, the ultimate underdog, to set the Israelites free, Moses's response was, "Who am I, that I should go to Pharaoh and bring the Israelites out of Egypt?" (Exodus 3:11). I think that is a fair reaction. Moses responds to his next step the same way we often do: *Who am I to do that?* The more Moses looked at himself, the more insecure he became. Over the next two chapters, he gave God a list of excuses why he couldn't. "I don't have the credibility, I don't have the ability, and I certainly don't have what it takes." Do you ever feel like that? As though you don't have the background, education, or experience? That you don't have the gifting, skills, or talent? Or you think you just don't have what it takes? Well, you're in good company.

We tend to think of Moses as this super-spiritual hero of the faith, but we forget that he started as an insecure shepherd. When God found him, he was running from his past, hiding in the desert. I don't think Moses even realized how insecure he really was. If we could have met Moses before his encounter with the burning bush, he probably would have bragged about how many sheep he had and how amazing they were. He probably would have let us see his trophies for being the best shepherd in the Midian valley five years in a row. He probably would have showed us his baby lambskin sandals that were the finest in fashion. We would have walked away thinking, *Man, that guy has it all together.* Moses was really good at hiding his insecurities in the things of this world, and so are we.

> Have you ever heard someone say, "God won't give you more than you can handle"? Well, I hate to break it to you, but that's a lie.

In fact, the harder we try to make other people think we have it all together, the more insecure we really are. But God has an interesting way of dealing with our hidden insecurities. He will place us in positions that perfectly expose them so he can make us secure. He will give us a job, a situation, a relationship, an invitation, or an assignment—a next step—that is perfectly designed to expose our insecurities because he loves us too much to let us stay in bondage.

Have you ever heard someone say, "God won't give you more than you can handle"? Well, I hate to break it to you, but that's a lie. It's a nice, churchy statement, but it's not true. God always gives you more than you can handle. Moses couldn't handle confronting the most powerful man on the face of the earth. The Israelites couldn't handle fighting a nation of giants. Paul couldn't handle writing most of the New Testament. God gave them way more than they could handle, and he will do the same with us. He will give us assignments bigger than ourselves to expose the insecurities we didn't even realize we had to help us become aware of him.

In other words, next steps free us from the greatest bondage of all: ourselves.

When Moses asked, "Who am I to do that?," God responded by saying, "I will be with you" (Exodus 3:12). That's a fascinating reply. At first it looked as if God didn't answer Moses's questions. But maybe he did. Maybe his answer is the foundation of our security. God's answer was, *Moses, you are the one I am with. Your security comes from my presence in your life.* Moses was looking at what was wrong with him instead of what was right with God. While he was standing in front of the burning bush, he was still focused on his problems instead of God's presence. So God said, *You want to know who you are? You are the one I am with. I am the Great I Am, and I will be everything you need me to be. What qualifies you to go is ME!*

God's response to Moses isn't unique. You will find this scenario throughout the Bible. When God gives someone an assignment bigger than themselves, their insecurities are revealed: *Who am I? I can't do this. Send someone else. Not me, Lord.* And God's response is almost always, *But I will be with you.* Whether it was Gideon, Jeremiah, or the disciples, God's response to their insecurities was, *You are the one I am with.*

When we ask, "Who am I to do that?," God doesn't respond with how great *we are;* he responds with how great *he is.* We want to talk about what's wrong with us, but God wants to talk about what's right with him. We want to tell God who we aren't, but he wants to tell us who he is. God's presence is your great qualifier. You are the one he is with!

Never Alone

One of the most significant promises God has given us is that he will always be wherever he asks us to go. In other words, God never sends us to do anything on our own. Even his name, Emmanuel, means "God with us" (Matthew 1:23). "The LORD himself goes before you and will be with you; he will never leave you nor forsake you. Do not be afraid; do not be discouraged" (Deuteronomy 31:8). God has given us the greatest gift of all—the gift of himself. With each step he asks us to take, he promises *he will* go before us. His presence prepares the way. He opens doors, releases provision, defeats our enemies, and empowers us with his authority. The cloud brings the super to our natural.

God continually reminds us, "Be strong and courageous. Do not be terrified; do not be discouraged, for the LORD your God will be with you wherever you go" (Joshua 1:9). His presence is the antidote for our insecurities. Only his presence can remove the fear and discouragement from our lives. If God is with you, who or what can be against you? For where his presence is, there his power resides. The unknown isn't scary when you know who is with you.

In the midst of life, the question we are all trying to answer is, where does my security come from? Does it come from our looks, money, abilities, relationships, status, or performance? Or does it come from the Lord? King David declared, "Some trust in chariots and some in horses, but we trust in the name of the LORD our God. They are brought to their knees and fall, but we rise up and stand firm" (Psalm 20:7–8). Insecurity is simply trusting in someone or something else to provide our security. And although other things may bring temporary confidence, what happens when we don't look like that anymore, when the money runs out, when our titles change, or when we get cropped out of the picture? Our security is determined by the reliability of the one we trust. Therefore, the only thing that will ever make us secure is *the One* who never changes.

TASTE AND SEE

For most of us, it's not until our inabilities are exposed that we begin to look for the one who is able. Therefore, every next step we are asked to take is an invitation to be aware of God's presence. The real question isn't, *Is God with us?* It's, *Are we aware of his presence?* But unfortunately, many of us don't really know much about the presence of God. No one has ever taught us about it, so we aren't really sure if we have ever experienced it. It's easy to say, "God is with me," as a theory or out of intellectual knowledge. But God's presence isn't information to know. He's a person to experience, and his name is Jesus.

God's presence is simply *our awareness that he is with us and that he is revealing himself to us.* And we need to be awakened to his personal presence in our lives. Here are some of the ways we are invited to experience his presence.

His presence holds us together. "In him all things hold to-gether" (Colossians 1:17). The presence of God is literally holding the fiber and fabric of the universe together. Right now his presence is holding the cells, molecules, and atoms of our bodies together. This book that you are holding in your hand is being held together by him. When it feels as though your job, marriage, or circumstances are flying apart, *are you aware* that his presence is holding your life together?

His presence surrounds us. "Where can I go from your Spirit? Where can I flee from your presence?" (Psalm 139:7). God goes before us, is behind us, and is all around us. There is no place we can go to get away from his presence. We are no longer lost because he says we are now found. When you are taking a next step, *are you aware* that his presence has already gone before you to prepare the way?

His presence is within us. Jesus "breathed on them and said, 'Receive the Holy Spirit'" (John 20:22). As followers of Jesus, we have the Spirit of the living God dwelling inside us. The same power that conquered the grave resides within and upon us. As we walk through life, we are never alone. When you step into a situation where you need wisdom, guidance, or power, *are you aware* that his presence is literally within you to provide everything you need?

His presence is in our godly relationships. "Where two or three come together in my name, there am I with them" (Matthew 18:20). Jesus says that when we gather with other believers, he comes to be with us. Whenever we get together in a small group or serving team or intentionally meet with other believers, there is a unique measure of God's presence among us. It's as if

Jesus himself pulled up a chair at the table. When you gather with your godly relationships, *are you aware* that Jesus himself has come to bring comfort, compassion, and hope?

His presence is tangible in our worship. God is "enthroned in the praises of Israel" (Psalm 22:3, NKJV). God always comes wherever he is welcomed. When we gather as a community of believers, our worship creates a throne for Jesus in the spiritual realm. Our corporate praise builds a throne for Jesus and invites him to take his place as king over our lives. He comes to rule and reign over our circumstances, fear, pain, and brokenness. When you worship, *are you aware* that your praise is bringing you into the throne room of heaven?

The presence of God is the greatest change agent in the universe, for "where the Spirit of the Lord is, there is freedom" (2 Corinthians 3:17). You need more than a cognitive understanding of his presence; you need an experience. You can intellectually know God is with you without ever experiencing that he is, so you are invited to "taste and see that the LORD is good" (Psalm 34:8). God gave the Israelites his constant presence through the cloud so that at any moment, they could look up and see his faithfulness, taste his provision, feel his power, and experience his goodness. The cloud never left the Israelites, and it'll never leave you. May you awaken to his presence and declare, "Surely the LORD is in this place, and I was not aware of it" (Genesis 28:16).

Faith is the belief that God is here even when you can't feel him.

So can you set this book down, close your eyes, and become aware that *HE is with you right now?* And if he is here, then all of the wisdom, comfort, love, and power of heaven is also here. Be still and know he is God. His presence is bigger than your circumstances.

BECOMING AWARE OF WHAT MATTERS

Until recently, I had always believed that when God led the Israelites out of Egypt, he was making a beeline to the Promised Land. After four hundred years of slavery, you would think everyone, including God, would be a bit anxious to get there. But the first place he led them wasn't to the Promised Land. Instead he led them to Mount Sinai and invited them to worship him.

"This is what the LORD says: Israel is my firstborn son. . . . *Let my son go, so he may worship me*" (Exodus 4:22–23). God wanted them to enjoy the Promiser before they enjoyed his promises. In his wisdom, he knew that if they went to the Promised Land without a heart of worship, they would turn his promises into idols, thereby unintentionally enslaving themselves again. So God went to great lengths to bring them to himself not for his good but for their good. "You yourselves have seen what I did to Egypt, and how I carried you on eagles' wings and *brought you to myself*" (19:4). And he has done the same for us. Like he did with the Israelites, God is always inviting us to worship him because worship keeps us free.

One of my concerns for today's church is that we have

overemphasized the sermon and underemphasized the presence of God. Like clockwork, every weekend, worship centers throughout the country fill up with people around the third song. There is a subtle belief that as long as we make it to the service in time for the sermon, then we "had church." We come late and skip "worship" because God's presence is often of little or no value to us. I know we are busy—it's hard to get our kids ready, it was probably a long week, and our favorite team is playing on TV. But we will always make time for what we value most. Church isn't about being entertained by a sermon; it's about encountering the living God. If we didn't meet with God, then we didn't *have church*. The sermon is not the main event; Jesus is. Too often, we enjoy what God does for us without enjoying God himself. And if sermons were enough, then the American church would be the healthiest most mature church in all of history.

I tell our church all the time, "If your life is so busy that you can't be here for a sixty-five-minute service, I would encourage you to come on time for worship and leave early instead of coming late and staying for the sermon." If we are so busy that we don't have sixty-five minutes to meet with God, then we don't need another sermon; we need to worship. We don't need more content; we need more connection. And that is what worship does: Worship reconnects the drifting heart to the Anchor of our souls. When we worship, we become free of our insecurities because we learn to become aware of the One who is with us. Only the heart that worships Jesus lives free. Only the heart that worships has the faith to follow the cloud.

The Gift of Desperation

For some reason, people tend to think that pastors are somehow different from the rest of the world. So I often laugh at the silly things people say to me, such as, "It must be nice to work only one day a week," and, "What's it like to have God answer all your prayers?" But the one that really gets me is, "It's so easy for you to get up there and preach." Really? Come on, man. Come hang out with me for a week. Every Sunday I have to get up and speak to thousands of people across multiple campuses and multiple services. I have six days to prepare something fresh that is anointed, relevant, engaging, and funny. Moses got forty days on the mountain to come back with his sermon—I get six.

Without question, preaching is one of the hardest things of my life. My biggest fear growing up as a kid was reading out loud in public. Every day in school I was terrified that the teacher would call on me to read in front of the class because I had a stuttering problem. In my nervousness, I would mispronounce almost every word while the entire class laughed. In fact, one of the worst grades I ever got was in preaching class in seminary. That's comforting, isn't it? And if that isn't bad enough, I am an introvert. Large groups of people exhaust me. I prefer the woods and solitude to platforms and crowds.

So every week it's the same cycle: *God, I don't know what to say. I can't do this. This is too much for me. Send someone else to do it. Preaching is more than I can handle.* But remember, we

already said that God will place us in positions that are perfectly designed to expose our insecurities. So every weekend
when I walk onto the platform, I am forced to look to him
because I know I don't have what it takes. Instead of looking
at my ability, I have to look to his power. Instead of focusing
on my struggles, I have to look to his strength. Every week I
have to stop and become aware that *he is with me.* My assignment frees me from myself and allows his power to be released
through my life. One of the hardest things in my life is actually one of the greatest gifts because it keeps me desperately
dependent upon Jesus.

While God might not ask you to confront Pharaoh or preach
every weekend, he will ask you to do something that makes you
wonder, *Who am I to do that?* God didn't need Moses to free the
Israelites. He doesn't need me to preach the gospel. And he doesn't
need you to take whatever step he is inviting you to take. But he
invites us to follow so we can become increasingly aware of him.
Next steps don't need us; we need them. And it's only in the step
you don't think you can take where you discover that he is greater
than your insecurities.

TREASURE AND CLAY

Do you remember when Jesus invited Peter to walk on the water?
That has to be one of the greatest stories in the Gospels. As Jesus
was calmly walking by the disciples' boat out in the middle of the
lake, Peter, in only the way he could, said " 'Lord, if it's you . . . tell

me to come to you on the water.' 'Come,' [Jesus] said" (Matthew 14:28–29). Talk about a next step. And in that moment, Peter had one of the greatest experiences of his life. While the rest of the disciples stayed comfortable in the boat, Peter intently looked to Jesus in the midst of the unknown. The disciples were so focused on their inability to defy physics that they remained within the safety of the boat. But as Peter's eyes were fixed on the Author and Perfecter of faith, the labels and limits of this world no longer defined him. He did the impossible. Yeah, Peter stumbled and got a little wet, but he walked on water! Jesus didn't let him sink.

And he won't let you sink.

The safest place you will ever be is when you are desperately dependent upon Jesus. It's always safer to walk on water with Jesus than to stay in the boat without him. That's why God is always inviting you to *come.* He wants you to get out of your safe boat of man-made security and walk on top of your insecurities—to face your biggest fears by looking into his face.

It's in the moments when we think we will sink that we discover that his presence gives us the strength to stand. The cloud loves to lead us where we have never been before so we can move from self-consciousness to God awareness. God's vision for your life is so big that it forces you to be desperate for his presence. In fact, if you are not desperate for his presence, your life is too small. If you can do everything in your life on your own, then you probably

> The safest place you will ever be is when you are desperately dependent upon Jesus.

aren't following the cloud. Like Moses, you may be hiding your insecurities in the things of this world, because it's often easier to hide our insecurities by staying in the spaces we can control than it is to follow him into the unknown. Yes, you might get a little wet, but until you walk on your insecurities with him, you have yet to experience the fullness of the freedom he offers.

> You will never believe that God is all you need until God is all you have.

I don't know about you, but I would rather walk on water and get wet than be a skeptic dry in the boat.

So my question for you is, what is God inviting you to do that you think you just can't? Maybe it's *I can't raise this child. I can't stay in this season. I can't be a leader. I can't share my faith. I can't make this change. I can't do this, go there, or say that.* It's in the moments where you say, "I can't," that you will most clearly hear him say, *I am with you.* His grace is sufficient for you, and his power is made perfect in your weakness. "We have this treasure in jars of clay to show that this all-surpassing power is from God and not from us" (2 Corinthians 4:7). He has placed his treasure in your clay. Our brokenness makes us believe that we aren't qualified or don't have what it takes. And although that may be true, he is and he does.

You will never believe that God is all you need until God is all you have.

Follow the Cloud—Live Free

God's grace places us in positions that perfectly expose our insecurities. What are two or three current areas in which you feel inadequate? What insecurities do those bring to the surface? What is God trying to say to you to bring you the security you need?

God is with us. That isn't just information; it is reality. How have you been aware of his presence in your life recently? Where have you "tasted and seen" that he is good? Have you shared that with anyone—family member, friend, spouse, child? If not, consider being a witness to the truth of Emmanuel: God with us.

RELEASE HIS KINGDOM

WHO YOU ARE DETERMINES WHAT YOU DO

10

HOW TO KILL A GIANT

Little by little I will drive them out before
you, until you have increased enough to
take possession of the land.

—Exodus 23:30

The giants never had a chance.

The truth is they never do. And after forty years of following the cloud, the Israelites finally believed it. The giants who currently inhabited the Promised Land (see Numbers 13:26–33) had been defeated the moment God promised the land to Abraham hundreds of years earlier, because no enemy can stand against the promises of God. Regardless of how loud the giants could roar, they already lost the battle before it had even begun.

I wonder what it would have been like for the Israelites to look across the Jordan River into the Promised Land. A powerless enemy occupied their home. Squatters wielding nothing more than the weapon of fear were infringing upon their inheritance. All the Israelites had to do was, by faith, take possession of what God had already given them: "I will give you every place where you set your foot" (Joshua 1:3). But they had stood on this shore once before. Unfortunately, doubt and unbelief turned a two-year journey into a forty-year one.

Sometimes it takes awhile for us to believe in the goodness of God.

But God is a God of second chances, and this time things were different. Throughout the years, the cloud led them to discover that they were beloved children with a good Father. Manna from heaven, water from a rock, protection in the desert, healing from diseases—every step helped change their thinking about who they were and who he was. As they received

> Sometimes it takes awhile for us to believe in the goodness of God.

their identity and experienced the goodness of the Father, they finally had the faith to follow. God's faithfulness yesterday gave them the faith they needed for today. Instead of looking at the size of the giants, this time they were focused on the size of their God. It was time for them to step into their purpose, destroy the works of darkness, and release God's kingdom throughout the land. And the same invitation is waiting for us.

It has always been God's plan to have man, made in his image and likeness, rule over creation. We are God's delegated authority on earth. He has empowered us to rule and reign on his behalf: "God blessed them and said to them, Be fruitful, multiply, and fill the earth, and subdue it [using all its vast resources in the service of God and man]" (Genesis 1:28, AMPC). We are commanded to *be fruitful,* bringing things to the fullness of their potential; *multiply,* reproducing the life of God in those around us; *fill the earth,* saturating our areas of influence with the knowledge of the glory of God; *subdue the world,* releasing God's goodness, order, and design into the chaos around us; and *use our resources,* bringing forth God's purposes in the lives of man.

We are on mission not *for him* but *with him* as co-laborers. As we discover who we are and who he is, we find the faith to do what we were created to do. Our restored identity releases a renewed purpose within our hearts. The forgiveness of Jesus always leads us to participate in the mission of God. Instead of striving to build our own little kingdoms on foundations of sinking sand, we are invited to a superior life of releasing his kingdom from a foundation of Rock.

As you look out over the horizon of your life, you are called, like the Israelites, to destroy the giants of darkness who have already been defeated. And the giants of disease, despair, poverty, chaos, brokenness, and evil don't have a chance. You have been empowered by love to stand in the face of fear. So don't let squatters steal your inheritance. Remember, you aren't fighting *for* victory; you are fighting *from* victory. In fact, Jesus said, "All authority in heaven and on earth has been given to me. Therefore go and make disciples of all nations" (Matthew 28:18–19). If Jesus has *all* authority, then the giants have *none.* Through you, God has destined *his kingdom come, his will be done on earth as it is in heaven* (see Matthew 6:10). So what are you waiting for?

Unlock the Treasure

As a kid, I loved to collect keys. There was always something mysterious about a ring full of old keys. The older the key, the more intrigue it had. I believed that each key held the potential to unlock hidden rooms and open secret treasures. Even though my keys were probably just for old toolboxes and storage closets, there was still something empowering about holding them in my hand. That's because keys hold the power to release the unseen. They are full of tremendous potential because keys represent authority and access.

Let's say I gave you a key to my house. In handing you my key, I would be giving you authority to access everything in my home whenever you wanted. You could unlock my door, go in, rest on my couch, get something from my fridge, play with my lacrosse stuff, or use my hunting gear. If I have entrusted you with my keys, then you have full authority to access what belongs to me.

Jesus said, "I will give you the keys of the kingdom of heaven; whatever you bind on earth will be bound in heaven, and whatever you loose on earth will be loosed in heaven" (Matthew 16:19). When Jesus gave us the keys to the kingdom, he empowered us with authority to access heaven and bring it to earth. He has given us unending access to that which belongs to him. As his followers, we have the authority to unlock the wisdom, compassion, healing, love, hope, power, and resources of heaven in any and every situation. But it takes faith to use the authority he has given us. Our identity is received, but our authority must be exercised. His keys don't belong in our pockets; they are to be used. All of creation is eagerly waiting for the children of God to use the keys that unlock the treasures of heaven. But our willingness to use them is always based on our revelation of who we are.

For example, my son is confident in his identity as my son and in our relationship together, so he never hesitates to use what belongs to me: "Hey, Dad, my friend Chad is hungry. I'm going to give him something to eat." "Dad, I used your tools to fix my bike." "Dad, I gave your Gatorade to the garbage man because he looked thirsty." He believes that everything I have is available to him, so he expects to use my resources to impact his world. The same is true with us.

When we are confident in our identity and our relationship with the Father, we will have the faith to release his kingdom: "Dad, my friend is sick. Let's heal her." "Dad, I used your stuff to provide what these hurting people need." "Dad, this is a hopeless situation, so I am going to give out some of your love." God is our Father, our Dad, and he has given us his keys. It's time to use them to serve the world.

SENT INTO THE WORLD

If you follow the cloud, you will quickly discover that it is always leading you into situations where you will need the keys of the kingdom. In fact, at the end of his life, Jesus prayed, "My prayer is not that you take them out of the world but that you protect them from the evil one. They are not of the world, even as I am not of it. . . . As you sent me into the world, I have sent them into the world" (John 17:15–16, 18). Okay, wait a second. Is that really in the Bible? I thought we were supposed to hide out in our Christian bubble until Jesus returns. Are you sure Jesus wants to send us into the world? Isn't that dangerous?

That verse runs counter to what many of us think Jesus would say. We are often trying to get out of the very world he is sending us into. But that's missing the point. The goal of Christianity is not about getting us to heaven someday; it's about bringing heaven to earth today.

> Like Jesus, we are anointed to do the unexpected wherever we are.

The cloud leads us into the world to release the goodness of God.

Jesus said, "As the Father has sent me, I am sending you" (John 20:21). We have drastically underestimated the depth of his statement. We aren't sent to be good religious people who spend their lives avoiding evil. We have been sent as beloved children empowered by our Father to destroy the works of the devil, to bring heaven to earth, and to reveal God's love to a fearful world. Like Jesus, we are anointed to do the unexpected wherever we are.

We are anointed—Jesus said, "The Spirit of the Lord is on me, because he has anointed me" (Luke 4:18). Jesus, the Son of Man, was anointed by the Holy Spirit to do great and mighty things. However, when we look at Jesus's example, it often feels unattainable for us. It's easy to think, *Well, of course he could do those things; he was the Son of God.* But what we forget is that

Jesus performed all of his miracles as a human man anointed by the Spirit of the living God. Acts 10:38 tell us, "God anointed Jesus of Nazareth with the Holy Spirit and power, and . . . he went around doing good and healing all who were under the power of the devil, because God was with him." Jesus walked this earth as a Spirit-filled man. He even said, "The Son can do nothing by himself" (John 5:19). His power came from the anointing of the Holy Spirit, not from his divine nature.

Do you know what that means? The same anointing and power Jesus had is now available to us. As we are filled with the same Holy Spirit, we are empowered to walk in the supernatural power and character of Jesus. He said, "I tell you the truth, anyone who has faith in me will do what I have been doing. He will do even greater things than these" (John 14:12). God won't ask you to do something he hasn't empowered you to do, so if he sends you like Jesus, he anoints you like Jesus.

To do the unexpected—Everywhere Jesus went, he did the unexpected. He stepped into people's lives and put the love of God on display. He touched the leper who was forced to live on the outskirts of town. He played with the children who were pushed to the side. He hugged the sinful woman who was full of shame. He brought the *opposite spirit* of whatever spirit was at work in each situation.

If there was hate, he brought love. If there was fear, he brought faith. If there was despair, he brought hope. If there was chaos, he brought peace. Why? Because darkness is defeated by the opposite spirit. Love overcomes hate. Faith overcomes fear. Hope overcomes despair. Peace overcomes chaos. Jesus said, "Go! I am sending you out like lambs among wolves" (Luke 10:3). Although that might sound scary, in the kingdom of God, the lamb defeats the wolf every time. A baby in a manger defeated the entire kingdom of darkness. One man on a cross conquered sin, death, and the grave.

Like Jesus, we are sent into this world with the opposite spirit to do the unexpected. We are salt and light bringing taste to a flavorless world and light into pitch-black darkness. If you are offended by your boss, instead of judging him or her, Jesus sends you to serve that person. If you are disappointed in your spouse, instead of pointing out his or her flaws, give encouragement. If there is a hostile person in your life, instead of responding with anger, come with the opposite spirit of kindness. Jesus sends you to do the unexpected.

For most of her life, Sharon lived a lifestyle contrary to Christianity. Because of the public hostility between her lifestyle and Christianity, most of the experiences she has had with Christians have been full of judgment and condemnation. So she hated Christians and she hated their Christ.

One day after a routine doctor appointment, Sharon was diagnosed with cancer and had to be immediately hospitalized. Sadly, because her life was full of broken relationships, she had no one to care for her during treatment. Loneliness is a sorrow the human heart was never meant to know.

So when Jenny, a woman from our church who worked with Sharon, heard about what happened, she went to visit Sharon in the hospital. Sharon had always disliked Jenny because she knew she was a Christian. You can imagine the awkwardness of that first visit when Jenny walked in. Sharon was lying in her hospital bed expecting the judgment speech she had heard from so many others before. Instead, Jenny walked in with flowers and balloons and said, "I'm so sorry you're sick. We really miss you at work."

Over the next few months, Jenny visited Sharon every week. She brought meals, fresh coffee, and magazines. They talked, laughed, and shared their stories. After a few months, Sharon's cancer went into remission and she was released from the hospital. When she got home, she called Jenny, the only friend she had, and nervously asked, "Would it be okay if I went with you to church next week? I would like to learn about *your* Jesus." It's amazing how kindness can soften even the hardest of hearts. So Sharon, who hated Christians, is now one of them because one person had the courage to bring the opposite spirit of love and do the unexpected.

Wherever we are—Jesus lived out his mission wherever he was. He did the unexpected on roads, in homes, at the temple, in the wilderness, on the water, and in the tomb. The Holy Spirit was with him, so he brought the Father's kingdom everywhere he went. The same is true for you.

Your ministry is wherever you are. You are an undercover soldier, an agent of the kingdom of heaven, sent behind enemy lines with the anointing to do the unexpected. Your cover is your job, your school, your position, your family, or your current season. Your assignment gives you unique access to bring the life of God to the people of this world.

If you're a delivery driver, every day God is sending you all over town to bring his hope to people's despair. If you're a teacher, every day you have the authority to speak life, believe the best, and invest in kids who have broken homes and broken hearts. If you're a businessperson, every day you get to show the world that God's ways are better than man's ways. If you're a stay-at-home parent, you can go to parks, games, activities, schools, and neighborhoods empowered to bring his peace into the chaos around you. You aren't just doing a job; you are releasing his kingdom. "I will give you every place where you set your foot" (Joshua 1:3).

Every day you have to remind yourself that *you are anointed to do the unexpected wherever you are!* "Greater is he that is in you, than he that is in the world" (1 John 4:4, KJV). In other words, the kingdom within you is superior to the giants around you. You are God's ambassador, sent with his authority to represent, or re-present, his love to a desperate world. But you can't give what you have yet to receive. "We love because he first loved us" (1 John 4:19). Only when you believe that you are beloved like Jesus is will you have the faith to be sent like Jesus was.

Big Things Start Small

As we talk about our purpose, the topic of destiny usually comes into the conversation. But I don't think we really know what to do with that word. I mean, when was the last time you thought about your destiny? We watch movies, hear inspirational stories, and listen to sermons that portray a sense of destiny that feels beyond our reach. And when that big word is carelessly thrown around, it often brings with it a sense of hopelessness because many of us feel as though we have already missed out on ours. Average jobs, struggling families, and mindless routines certainly don't seem like inspiring destinies.

But maybe we have overcomplicated it.

Destiny is not about finding tomorrow; it's about walking with God today. It's not a destination; it's a way of life. Your destiny is found in a thousand little steps, not in one giant leap. It's not about one moment of divine favor; it's a lifetime of trusting God. Destiny is simply seizing the divine opportunities that come every single day. Every time we step into the spaces that glorify God and awaken our hearts, we are living our destinies. "'For I know the plans I have for you,' declares the LORD, 'plans to prosper you and not to harm you, plans to give you hope and a future'" (Jeremiah 29:11). God's plan is that you would embrace the now, full of hope for the future.

For example, David didn't just wake up one day and decide to go kill Goliath. His entire life had been preparing him for that moment. For years, he was faithful to take each step that came his way. He learned to think like a giant killer long before he ever killed one. "Your servant has been keeping his father's sheep. When a lion or a bear came and carried off a sheep from the flock, I went after it, struck it and rescued the sheep from its mouth. . . . Your servant has killed both the lion and the bear; this uncircumcised Philistine will be like one of them" (1 Samuel 17:34–36). In every situation, David had the faith to bring forth the goodness of God. He was faithful, *full of faith,* in the little

> Destiny is not about finding tomorrow; it's about walking with God today.

steps, so God entrusted him with greater steps. Whether it was submitting to his father, serving as a lowly shepherd, killing a lion, or chasing a bear, all of those seemingly disconnected steps ultimately led him to the battlefield with Goliath. David understood that destiny isn't an epic moment in time but rather a way of life. His willingness to embrace today positioned him to find tomorrow.

While we all want to become giant killers, we just aren't sure we want to take the steps that prepare us for battle. But to say no to the now is to say no to the future. Giant killers always start as lowly shepherds. Instead of complaining about their circumstances, they embrace them. Glancing through the Bible, we find that every major leader was faithful in the *little* long before they were entrusted with *much.* Joshua was Moses's servant for forty years, Nehemiah was a cupbearer to the king, Timothy was Paul's assistant, and Jesus was a carpenter for thirty years. Every day, they brought God's goodness into their current assignments. They saw kingdom purpose where others saw mundane routines.

> Big people embrace small tasks because small tasks create big people.

Maybe we can learn from their example.

Big people embrace small tasks because small tasks create big people. It's only in the pasture where God can prepare you for the palace. Whether you're a stay-at-home parent, a student, unemployed, in a job you love, or in a season you can't stand, your destiny is releasing his kingdom in the here and now.

THE RIPPLE EFFECT OF FAITH

Think about it like this: heaven comes to earth with every step you take. My friend Kyle's eighth birthday is a great example.

Every year his birthday celebration was extra special because the doctors had said he would never see his first. Kyle was born with cerebral palsy and a number of genetic disorders that left him confined to a wheelchair.

One of the many struggles Kyle's family faced was placing him and his wheelchair into their old van. Two hundred thousand miles, no air conditioning in the Texas heat, and no way to comfortably get Kyle in and out of the van—made daily life a significant challenge. But this year a special birthday gift was waiting. One family's next step was about to become another family's miracle.

I'll never forget the moment when Kyle's family became undone as they were handed the keys to a brand-new wheelchair-accessible van complete with hydraulics, ramps, lifts, and air conditioning. It was an extravagant gift they could never have afforded on their own—a gift that completely changed their lives. And it was all because one anonymous family decided to use what they had to release the life of God into that situation. That one step raised the faith level of our entire church.

Simply put, divine steps release heavenly life. If the "kingdom of God is within you" (Luke 17:21), every step you take releases God's kingdom into the world around you. The kingdom within you will ultimately become the kingdom around you. In the same way a boat leaves a giant wake behind it as it moves through the water, our lives leave a wake of life as we move with the cloud. The ripple effect of our obedience touches the lives of people on the shore who we might never even see. Our next steps aren't always about us. Sometimes they are simply about releasing God's power through our lives. Our next step might be someone else's miracle. If God's kingdom is within us, then wherever we bring his rule, his life will reign. That's why simple obedience always brings significant breakthrough.

I used to have a pastor who would ask, "How much will your sin cost me?" He wanted us to understand that our choices affect those around us. He had this little phrase: "Sin will take you further than you want to go, keep you longer than you want to stay, and cost you more than you want to pay." And although that's true, it's not very life-giving, is it? We are changed by love and grace, not shame and condemnation. If God is love, then fear is never a motivator in his kingdom.

> Simple obedience always brings significant breakthrough.

So what if we flipped it? What if we asked, "How much will your obedience bless me?" Or "How much will my next step bless others?" Maybe a better phrase is, *Faith will take you further than you thought you could go, free you faster than you thought you could be freed, and release through you more than you thought you could give.*

You are commissioned to be a life-giver. Not all of us can give a van, but we each have a next step. I wonder who will be touched by the wakes of life set in motion by your faith.

Answered Prayer

I'm not sure we will ever understand how significant our steps really are. Each step the cloud leads us to take is part of God's plan of establishing his kingdom on this earth. For example, when God first came to Moses, he said, "I have indeed seen the misery of my people. . . . I have heard them crying out . . . and I am concerned about their suffering. . . . So now, go. I am sending you" (Exodus 3:7, 10). God said, *Moses, you are my answer to their prayer, so go put my love on display.* One man's steps were designed to set an entire nation free.

That is a great picture of our lives in God's kingdom. God loves to tap us on the shoulder and say, *Hey, you see that person? Yeah, the one right there. I have seen his misery, I have heard his cry, and I am concerned about his suffering. He has a story you know nothing about. Now, go. You are my answer to his prayer.*

Kingdom people are God's answers to the world's prayers. Once you have been delivered, you become a deliverer. God doesn't say, "Now sit here and watch what I can do." He says, "Now go and watch what I will do through you." The kingdom of God operates on this simple premise: God does extraordinary things through ordinary people. He is glorified when his power is released through our weakness. We should never underestimate what God can do in and through a surrendered human heart.

I always smile when people come up to me and passionately point out a problem, opportunity, or need and say, "Somebody should really do something about that." My response is always the same: "You're right; *you should!* I am so glad you are going to take care of it. Please let me know how it goes." Usually they make a little frowny face and just walk away.

News flash! The reason you noticed that person or that need is because God is drawing your attention to it. The cloud is inviting you to be his answer to that problem. You are Jesus's outreach strategy. And the greatest miracles you will ever see are in the lives of the people you have yet to meet. You can't say, "Well, I don't have that gift," because releasing the kingdom isn't a gift; it's your calling. What needs do you see? What burdens your heart? What has captured your attention? That's someone else's prayer that God wants to answer through you.

At Valley Creek, we say we are more like Home Depot than like Burger King. We believe church is "You can do it; we can help," not "Have it your way." Church is where we are equipped with a renewed mind, a healthy heart, and skillful hands to partner with God in seeking and saving the lost. It's a training center where we are equipped, not a resort where we are entertained.

Ministry was never meant to be reserved for the elite; it's intended to be released to the masses. If Jesus entrusted fishermen, tax collectors, and zealots to lead his kingdom, why wouldn't he entrust students, rookies, and ordinary people?

Why wouldn't he entrust you?

May we never stop believing in the redemptive potential of humanity.

We must always remember that God has entrusted his people with his kingdom. In fact, even though I may never have met you, I believe you are a kingdom leader. You might not feel like a leader.

You might not believe you are a leader. You might not even be living as a leader. But think about it:

- *You have been made in God's image and likeness (see Genesis 1:26).*
- *You have everything you need through his divine power (see 2 Peter 1:3).*
- *You have been empowered with his authority (see Matthew 28:18–20).*
- *You have the Spirit of the living God within you (see Acts 1:8).*
- *You are the head and not the tail (see Deuteronomy 28:13).*
- *You are an influencer, not the influenced (see Matthew 5:13–14).*

That is just a portion of your redemptive potential. In Jesus, you have the potential to create, build, inspire, heal, restore, speak life, release hope, influence, and lead! And that potential is released with every next step you take. When you follow the cloud, you become a leader in this world, making the invisible visible, bringing his kingdom into the here and now. Good leaders are simply great followers, and that is your destiny.

Follow the Cloud—Live Free

Think of who comes to mind when you read this statement: "Big people embrace small tasks because small tasks create big people." What are some of the small steps God is asking you to take that you feel are meaningless or boring or below your ability? Remember, in the kingdom, faithfulness matters and commitment counts. Each step is a part of your destiny.

God has commissioned you to rule and reign on this earth with him. You are a kingdom leader. Do you believe that? Why or why not? If you are a kingdom leader, how would that change the way you live each day? Ask God to give you the faith to release his life into the world around you.

11

PIONEERS

Apathy is kryptonite to a cloud follower—at least it is to me.

Although there are a lot of things I can handle in life, apathy is usually not one of them. Apathetic people can sap my heart the way a piece of kryptonite could sap Superman's strength. *Faster than a speeding bullet! More powerful than a locomotive! Able to leap tall buildings in a single bound! It's Superman!* That is, until you pull out a little green rock and Superman becomes a super-wimp, helplessly crumpled on the ground, unable to move. That's how I feel when I am around apathetic people: the guy whose arms are crossed during an entire worship service, the person who refuses to celebrate when someone else is baptized, the woman who doesn't think she needs to take a next step, the person whose highest value is personal comfort. I would much rather have to temper desire than inspire indifference. I far prefer Peter's unbridled passion to the Pharisees' complacency.

Simply put, an apathetic Christian is someone who has settled for eternal life someday instead of abundant life today. Like kryptonite, their apathy has the power to drain the life from everyone who is exposed to it. And if the apathy of others never

bothers you, you might be apathetic!

> An apathetic Christian is someone who has settled for eternal life someday instead of abundant life today.

Apathy is a chronic heart disease we were never meant to have. It's a spirit of indifference that causes us to miss the life right in front of us. Apathy steals our present and hides our future. It's a contagious perspective that, maybe more than anything else, inhibits us from following the cloud. The apathetic believe, *This is as good as it gets,* while cloud followers believe, *The best is yet to come.*

Jesus confronted the apathetic heart when he said, "I know all the things you do, that you are neither hot nor cold. I wish that you were one or the other! But since you are like lukewarm water, neither hot nor cold, I will spit you out of my mouth!" (Revelation 3:15–16, NLT). Jesus's words are so strong because apathy is the birthplace of religion. Remember, activity is not an indication of life, and busyness is not a sign of passion. God doesn't care how good your external life looks; he cares how alive your heart is, because the condition of your heart will determine the quality of your life (see Proverbs 4:23).

Sadly, life hasn't turned out the way many of us expected. Without even realizing it, we have become disillusioned, skeptical, or tired. As we have been hurt by life, we have built walls of stone around our hearts of flesh. Divorce, abortion, abuse, trauma, abandonment, death, unmet expectations, and disappointment have all contributed to our self-protection. It's hard to find a soft heart in an old body. The only problem is that the same walls that keep us from getting hurt again also keep us from receiving love. If pain can't get in, then neither can love. Our attempt at self-protection has actually become a self-imposed prison. So over time, our hearts become numb. And a numb heart will always create an apathetic life. But Jesus didn't give you a new heart so you could spend your life numbing it.

Jesus said, "The thief comes only to steal and kill and destroy; I have come that they may have life, and have it to the full" (John 10:10). Satan wants to steal your affection, kill your heart, and destroy your faith. But Jesus has come to resurrect your life by healing your heart. And only a whole heart can live a passionate life.

> Jesus didn't give you a new heart so you could spend your life numbing it.

YOU GO FIRST

Ever since I was a kid, I have loved the passion of pioneers. The stories of Lewis and Clark, Ernest Shackleton, and Jacques Cousteau have always inspired me. In fact, I even wanted to have the word *pioneer* in my church plant that never happened. There is something about pioneering the unknown that captivates the human heart. Maybe it's because we were created to discover the unknown and bring order to the chaos beyond the horizon (see Genesis 1:28). And although pioneers' adventures are all different, they all have one thing in common. They have to be willing to push through the naysayers around them and be willing to go first regardless of what anyone else thinks.

One of the greatest barriers you will ever face in following the cloud is the apathy of those around you. As I have followed the cloud, I have learned that I can't let other people's apathy keep me from my destiny. For example, the apathy of ten spies who originally explored the Promised Land prevented the entire nation from following the cloud. "They spread among the Israelites a bad report about the land they had explored. They said, 'The land we explored devours those living in it. All the people we saw there are of great size'" (Numbers 13:32). So the Israelites grumbled saying, "Our brothers have made us lose heart" (Deuteronomy 1:28). God was inviting them to step into their purpose, but the apathy of ten men was like kryptonite and stole the future of more than a million people. The cloud was drawing them to come and see the wonders of the kingdom, but the apathy of man was driving them back to Egypt.

I wonder how often that describes our lives. How many women want to passionately follow Jesus but don't because of their husband's apathy? How many students want to follow the cloud but don't because of their parents' apathy? How many men want to honor God in the marketplace but don't because of the

> One of the greatest barriers you will ever face in following the cloud is the apathy of those around you.

apathy of their coworkers? How many people want to passionately worship in church but don't raise their voices or their hands because of the apathy of those around them?

Satan will use the apathy of others to suppress your passion. It's like a bucket of cold water on your hot flame. But no one has the authority to steal your passion. Their complacency has only the power you give it.

A simple truth we need to hide in our hearts is, *I can't let your view of God determine my response to him*. Moses refused to allow the constant rebellion of the Israelites determine his response to God. The disciples refused to allow the crowd's rejection of Jesus determine how they responded to him. And if you are going to follow the cloud, you can't let the view of others determine your response to God.

Personally, I have struggled with this. When I first got into ministry, I just assumed that people wanted to passionately follow Jesus. I mean, why on earth would you be in church if you had no intent to walk with God?

But I quickly realized that not everyone was all that interested in taking next steps. Many people are just looking for their *next stop*. So for a season, the apathy of "Christians" caused me to question God. Their unwillingness to passionately follow him made me start to wonder, *Does the gospel even work? Where is the power of God? Is following him really worth it?* Their apathy was unraveling my faith. But then I realized that whether people are passionate about him or apathetic toward him, he is still God. Regardless of how anyone responds, he is still "the LORD, the

LORD, the compassionate and gracious God, slow to anger, abounding in love and faithfulness" (Exodus 34:6). In a world of apathy, he is worthy of my passion.

But passion always comes with a cost.

By definition, passion is simply that which you are willing to suffer for. For example, if you are passionate about the Dallas Cowboys, you are willing to suffer through a whole lot of heartbreaking fourth-quarter losses. If you are passionate about working out, you are willing to suffer through 5:00 a.m. workouts while the rest of us are sleeping. And if you are passionate about Jesus, you will have to suffer through the apathy of others without allowing it to make you apathetic. "For Christ's love compels us" to passionately follow him regardless of anyone else (2 Corinthians 5:14). Although hype is man-motivated and man-maintained, passion is Spirit-inspired and Spirit-sustained. Therefore, cloud followers always go first, even if they have to go alone.

IT'S A PARTY

If you did a top-ten list of the most-often-asked questions in church, I would bet the number one question would be "What's God's will for my life?" We desperately want to know God's will. Unfortunately, that question often paralyzes us. We can become so afraid of missing God's elusive will for our spouses, jobs, futures, callings, and lives that we end up not doing anything at all. Fear of making the wrong decision often keeps us from making any decision. So maybe we've been asking the wrong question.

Maybe a better question is "What has God already empowered me to do, and am I doing it?"

God has already empowered you to make disciples, be his ambassador, serve those around you, forgive those who have hurt you, be generous, and release his kingdom. God's will is that you would do what he has already invited you to do. Too often, we are waiting for God to move, but the truth is he is usually waiting for us to surrender. If we will value what's been revealed, he will show us what's hidden. If we will honor the revelation (what he has already asked us to do), he will uncover the mystery (the rest of his will for our lives). We need to be more concerned with what he *has said* than with what he *has yet to say*. That's how we follow the cloud.

I am convinced that a lot of us are bored in life because we are sitting on the sidelines watching others advance the kingdom. We are bored because instead of taking next steps we are watching other people live out their purpose. But we don't have tickets to the stadium; we have uniforms for the game. We were created to paint, draw, write, build, heal, restore, redeem, proclaim, worship, multiply, rule, and reign. We were created to walk into the unknown with the God who wants to be known. There is a pioneering spirit within us just waiting to be released. It's in our nature because we were made in the image and likeness of the One who always goes first.

If we are bored, maybe it's because we aren't really following him. If our lives are boring, then maybe we have unintentionally become religious. I am not saying we don't go to church. I am not saying we aren't doing "Christian things." I am not even saying we don't believe in God. However, if we are bored, we probably aren't actually following Jesus. Think about it. The Gospels paint a picture of a God who was the life of the party. Jesus says that signs and wonders will follow those who follow him (see Mark 16:17–18). He sends us to preach the kingdom, heal the sick, raise the dead, cast out demons, and cleanse the lepers (see Matthew 10:7–8). A Spirit-led life is anything but boring.

The Israelites weren't bored expanding the kingdom, killing giants, and taking the Promised Land. Peter wasn't bored walking on water, sharing his story, and healing the sick. Paul wasn't bored confronting demons, raising people from the dead, and planting churches all over the world. People who walk with Jesus don't have time to be bored because they are too busy releasing the kingdom. Their lives are full of stories worth telling. Is yours? If not, it's never too late to start following the cloud.

THE DANGER OF SUCCESS

My friends Justin and Dorise are great examples of cloud followers with a story to tell. Good jobs and nice paychecks allowed them to do what they wanted when they wanted. They had exactly what most of us spend our lives pursuing: worldly success. But as he often does, God had different plans. As the cloud started to move, my friends couldn't deny that God was inviting them to sell their business, move to a new city, and start our church's first multisite campus. So they were faced with a choice: ignore the thunderous whisper, or follow God into something that would change everything.

Although they were open to God's invitation, letting go of *their success* was the one thing holding them back. Some steps require more trust than others. There is nothing reasonable about selling a business in the middle of one's life and starting a new career. But only in giving everything up would they be able to find everything they were really looking for. So instead of holding on to what they had acquired, they opened their hearts to receiving what God offered. And just a few short years later, their willingness to be pioneers is now awakening an entire city. The campus is thriving, they are freer than they have ever been, and countless lives have been affected by the love of Jesus. Sure, they may have less money now, but they have more life! They discovered that a life of passionate purpose provides what a life of personal comfort never will. A discovery many people never make.

Playing it safe is often what keeps us from moving forward. The more established our lives become, the more we resist change. In fact, the great danger of success is fear of losing what we have gained. The more we have acquired, the more we become afraid of losing what we have. We are afraid to risk our possessions, tenure, seniority, comfort, security, paycheck, reputations, and safety. And when we are afraid to risk what we have, we start to allow divine opportunities to pass us by. So instead of passionately following God into the unknown, we spend our lives protecting what we already have.

And you know it's true, because I bet before you had anything, you were willing to take risks. When you had nothing to lose and everything to gain, it was easy to jump into divine opportunities. But somewhere along the way, success changed all of that.

The paradox is that the things we have spent our lives pursuing become the very things that keep us from moving forward.

Success has a way of unintentionally creating apathy in our hearts. Without even realizing it, our blessings can actually make us apathetic when we are afraid of losing them. So is that really success? To be enslaved by the very things you have been trying to acquire.

> It's always safer where God tells you to go than where fear tells you to flee.

Success is meant to inspire a life full of dreams, not take them from you. God doesn't want you to spend your life protecting your present, he wants you to follow him into your future. But you have to be willing to risk what you have to discover what God has in store. Remember, it's always safer where God tells you to go than where fear tells you to flee.

ADVANCE

Even though we may be full of a thousand good intentions, remember, it is direction, not intention, that determines our destiny. There is no such thing as neutral in the kingdom of God. You are moving either forward or backward. You are either following or drifting. You are either pioneering or settling. Unfortunately, there is no pause button in life.

I often hear people say things like, "I know I'm not really following Jesus, but I'm not really doing anything bad. I'm not taking any next steps, but I am not sinning either. I'm just kind of in neutral." Well, God says, "Anyone, then, who knows the good he ought to do and doesn't do it, sins" (James 4:17). In other words, it's sin to pass on divine opportunities. I mean why would we take a pass on the very purpose we were created for? The goal of the Christian life is not about playing it safe; it's about going for it for God's glory. Life is not about how much evil we can avoid; it's about how much love we can release. We were never meant to idle in neutral; we were called to shift into drive. And the problem with neutral is that it deceives us into thinking we are actually living. A day turns into a week, a week turns into a month, a month turns into a year, a year turns into years, and before we know it, years become a lifetime of missed opportunity and unrealized potential.

Think of your favorite football team again. Let's say it's the fourth quarter. Your team is up by a few points and there are only a few minutes left in the game. Your team has the ball, but instead of trying to score, they go into a defensive posture and just try to hold on to their lead. All they want to do is run the clock out and get

> Life is not about how much evil we can avoid; it's about how much love we can release.

into the locker room. Instead of playing *to win,* they start playing *not to lose.* The announcer usually chimes in and says, "If all they do is play defensively, they are going to lose this game. They better not stop playing offense, because the other team isn't going to quit until this is over." And what happens? The other team gets the ball and scores a touchdown, and your team loses every single time (or at least my team does). You can't just hold on, play defense, and expect to win. And yet that is what we often do.

Far too many of us just want to hold on and play defense. We want to hold on to what we have, avoid risk, and run the clock out. Instead of playing to win, we start playing not to lose. But you will always lose whatever you try to hold on to. Just ask the man who buried his one talent (see Matthew 25:14–30). The kingdom of God cannot advance with its people in retreat. Jesus never invites us to play defense; he only invites us to play offense. "I will build my church, and the gates of Hades will not overcome it" (Matthew 16:18). We are on offense, and all of hell can't stop us. No man can tear down that which Jesus is building. But if we hold back to try to hold on, we will miss out on life.

Again, just look at the Israelites. When they finally entered the Promised Land, their journey was far from complete. It wasn't time to kick back and coast; it was time to take the land. God told them, "Little by little I will drive [the nations of giants] out before you, until you have increased enough to take possession of the land" (Exodus 23:30). The Israelites were commanded to continue to take next steps. Either they were going to increase and advance or the giants were—it was their choice.

We can hear the echo of our created purpose in God's command to the Israelites. "Be fruitful and multiply; fill the earth and subdue it" (Genesis 1:28, NKJV). Whether it was Adam and Eve in the Garden of Eden, Noah after the Flood, the Israelites in the Promised Land, the disciples in the book of Acts, or you in your daily life, we are called to start right where we are and advance little by little, replacing the works of darkness with the life of God.

Cloud followers understand that there is always a next step. There is always more ground to take. There is always a new trail to blaze. Whether it's in their homes, relationships, neighborhoods, work, or school, they understand that missional living is their mandate. They take next steps to create space so other people can take theirs. They choose to be faithful in *their little,* knowing that is the key to being entrusted with *his much.* They know they are kingdom servants called to increase and advance for the glory of God.

Circle 3 Living

While we are called to be people who advance, we must never forget that when Jesus first called the disciples, he invited them to become someone, not do something. " 'Come, follow me,' Jesus said, 'and *I will make you fishers of men'* " (Matthew 4:19). He knew that a vision to become someone was far superior to a vision to do something. From the very beginning, Jesus invited them to a lifestyle of next steps, knowing that with each step they took, they would become Jesus-focused, Spirit-filled, life-giving people. Jesus knew that who we are becoming is infinitely more important than what we are doing, because when you become the right person, you will naturally do the right things. Identity determines purpose. As we have already said, fish swim, birds fly, cows moo, dogs bark, and followers of Jesus engage in the mission of Jesus. The wrong root will never produce the right fruit.

I think the church has often lost sight of this. Much of what we hear today in Christianity is about all the things "we have to do for God." So we spend our lives trying to give, serve, help, perform, and change, but no matter how much we do, we never feel as if we can ever do enough. We get stuck in the cycle of performance. We start at circle 3 and *do* in order to become, not realizing that Jesus has already *done* so that now in him we have already become. True circle 3 living—a godly life of purpose participating in the mission of God—is available only to those who

> Who we are becoming is infinitely more important than what we are doing.

have first received his grace and experienced his presence. You will never have the faith to live a kingdom life until you first believe you are a child of the King.

This is the pattern you see all throughout Scripture.

"Jesus went up on a mountainside and called to him those he wanted, and they came to him. He appointed twelve—*designating them apostles* [identity, circle 1]—*that they might be with him* [relationship, circle 2] *and that he might send them out to preach and to have authority to drive out demons* [purpose, circle 3]" (Mark 3:13–15, italics added).

God always starts his engagement with us in circle 1. He changes our identity, draws us into relationship with him, and *then* sends us to go and do *from* approval, not *for* it (see Genesis 1:26; Ezekiel 36:24–27; 2 Corinthians 5:17–20). Our purpose always starts with what he has done, not with what we have to do.

Before God asks us to do anything, he will always start by showing us he has already done everything. He will remind us that we are new creations before he asks us to live a new lifestyle. Who we now are changes what we used to do.

Butterflies no longer crawl in the mud; they soar in the sky.

What I have learned is that we don't get people to participate in the mission of God by telling them they have to; we lead people to the mission of God

> We are drawn by grace, not driven by expectations.

by reminding them of who they now are. We are drawn by grace, not driven by expectations. Therefore, only those who receive his grace and experience his presence will be passionate about releasing his kingdom. And only those who release his kingdom are fully alive.

People in bondage can't lead others to freedom, but slaves who have been set free will spend their lives passionately helping others find freedom. Circle 3 living is "I do this because of what the LORD did for me when I came out of Egypt" (Exodus 13:8).

It's time to pioneer.

Follow the Cloud—Live Free

Whose passion inspires you to follow Jesus? Whose apathy causes you to pull back? Do you think the way you live your life inspires people to follow, or does it discourage them and cause them to pull back?

The great danger of success is fear of losing what has been gained. What are you afraid of losing right now? Be as specific as you can. God has called you to increase and advance. What is God asking you to let go of? What is he asking you to grab ahold of?

12

ALL IN

As we pulled into a remote parking lot on the edge of a river in nowhere Alaska, we could hear the roar of the thirty-nine-degree water ripping down the canyon. The adults of my extended family had decided to go on an Alaskan adventure vacation. Instead of resting on a beach somewhere, we chose to go do a bunch of adventurous things together, and white-water rafting was at the top of our list.

After we signed our lives away on waivers, the river guides handed each of us a dry suit, helmet, and life jacket. As we were getting suited up, they began to give us our safety instructions. But I kind of stopped listening when I saw our boats pull out into the river, float about a hundred yards downstream, and pull up on the opposite shore. I tuned back in just in time to hear the guide say, "The river is at flood stage, and the water is so powerful that we need to make sure you can swim before we get started. So if you want to go rafting, you have to jump in the river and swim to the boats on the other side."

At that point, a bunch of strangers in our group said, "We're out." Half the group quit before we even started. But, hey, you only live once, so we took big breaths, jumped in, and swam as fast as we could across the rushing current. And we quickly found out that the dry suits weren't really dry!

We climbed into our boats, and the guide said, "There are two major stretches of rapids we will go through. After the first stretch, there is only one spot where you can get out. If you don't get out there, you will have to ride the river all the way to the bottom. But don't worry. I'll be with you, and this will be the ride of your life."

As the canyon started getting narrower, the water started getting rougher. Our little boat began bouncing off boulders, spinning in whirlpools, and submerging under giant waves. At the guide's commands, we paddled left and right, forward and backward, trying to avoid rocks, trees, and other obstacles. It was intense. And it was incredible.

As we exited the first stretch of rapids into calm water, we were all cheering with excitement. While we were giving each other high fives, thrilled that we had made it through, the guide shouted above the roar, "Okay, here is the one place you can get out before the second stretch of rapids. That was the warm-up stretch. It's about to get wild. Does anyone want to get out?"

My mom and Colleen instantly made eye contact and mouthed to each other, "Do you want to get out? Because I want to get out. I don't want to fall in. I'll get out if you get out."

They shouted, "We want to get out!"

Instantly, our entire family used the power of peer pressure. "You can't get out. Boooooo. Come on, keep going."

"We have to use the bathroom," one of them said.

Someone replied, "Well, the dry suit ain't dry anyways. You may as well just *go* in it. You know someone else already has."

Again, the guide said, "Does anyone want to get out? I need to know right now. This is your last chance."

Our peer pressure worked, and my mom and Colleen said, "Okay, we're in."

"All right, you are *all in* to the bottom of the canyon. Here we go," the guide said.

We floated around the corner and past the exit, and as I looked down the canyon into the second stretch of rapids, I thought, *I should've gotten out!*

As soon as we hit the white water, we were like a Lego man in a washing machine. The river tossed us around mercilessly. Our rubber boat uncontrollably rushed toward a giant boulder, and as we hit it head-on, I watched as Colleen was launched about twenty feet into the air. It all seemed to happen in slow motion. *Nooooooooo.* As she was flying through the air, her eyes locked on mine and she had an *"I'm going to kill you"* look on her face. She splashed into the water, and the river instantly swept her away. All we could see was her yellow helmet bobbing up and down in the white water passing in between giant boulders. As we were frantically paddling toward her in thirty-nine-degree water, I thought to myself, *I hope she peed in the suit.*

Finally, we maneuvered close enough for my brother to grab Colleen's life jacket and pull her back into the boat. My sigh of relief quickly turned into the realization that this was going to be the worst night in a hotel that we'd ever had.

As we paddled to the shore at the bottom of the canyon, I was terrified to make eye contact with her. But she totally surprised me with a huge smile and said, "That was *amazing*!"

Her fear of falling in was what actually made it an adventure of a lifetime. But had she gotten out halfway, taken a selfie and posted it online, she would have missed the whole thing. The same is true with following the cloud.

Too often we are willing to follow the cloud just enough to say we have tried it. We take a safe or convenient next step. Maybe we get saved, go to church, or give a little money, but as we look down the second stretch of rapids, where it gets wild, we think it's time to get out.

But you will never know what following Jesus is really like until you go *all in*. I think one of the saddest verses in the Bible is "From this time many of his disciples turned back and no longer followed him" (John 6:66). It's a verse full of missed opportunity. These disciples, who are only remembered for going halfway, were willing to go through the first stretch of rapids, but they got out before the real adventure began.

Jesus never invites us to get out halfway; he invites us only to go all in—to go for it, with him. "If anyone would come after me, he must deny himself and take up his cross and follow me. For whoever wants to save his life will lose it, but whoever loses his life for me and for the gospel will save it" (Mark 8:34–35). It's only when we get to the end of ourselves that we find the beginning of life. Simply stated, when we finally give up control, we step into the fullness of life. Only those who are *all in* will experience *all of life*.

When the river of God is flowing, don't ask questions; just jump in. Jesus is inviting you to move from ankle deep to knee deep to waist deep, until you can no longer touch the bottom (see Ezekiel 47). He is drawing you to keep following him one next step at a time until you fall overboard into his re-

> It's only when we get to the end of ourselves that we find the beginning of life.

lentless love and are fully submerged in the springs of Living Water. You can get out and play it safe, or you can jump in and live. Don't let fear keep you from the life God has for you. You were never meant to have a life full of *what-ifs*; you were meant to live a life full of *he is and he has*. The tide is rising; it's time to leave the safety of the shore and be swept away by his mercy and goodness.

We ask, "What if I fail?" But God asks, *"Do you want to become free?"*

FAITHFUL TO THE END

You won't always like where the cloud is leading you.

I'm sure the Israelites got tired of the endless wilderness and the sand in the desert. I would guess that David had enough of running and hiding from Saul. I bet the disciples grew weary of never knowing where they were going to sleep at night. And I'm sure you are tired of some of the things you have been walking through.

I know I am.

Our daughter, Emma Joy, was born with a life-altering, incurable disease. She has a rare autoimmune disorder that causes her body to attack itself. For years, with broken hearts, we have watched her struggle through immense physical pain.

It's hard to overstate the impact this has had on our family. We have pursued healing in every way possible. We have tried everything from modern medicine to radical diets to holistic natural health care to cutting-edge innovations. We have prayed, prophesied, declared, and anointed her with oil.

But she has *yet* to be healed.

To be honest, there are some days where Colleen and I think we can't make it one more day. Days where we are tired and discouraged. Days where we don't want to take any more steps. Days where we are done with the cloud.

But it's in those moments that we most clearly see the faithfulness of God. It's in the moments of desperation where we discover that we are never alone. "The LORD your God, who is going before you, will fight for you, as he did for you in Egypt, before your very eyes, and in the desert. There you saw how the LORD your God carried you, as a father carries his son, all the way you went until you reached this place" (Deuteronomy 1:30–31). Every time we stop and look back, we see his faithfulness. Every sleepless night. Every ER visit. Every doctor's appointment. Every time we have cried until we had no tears left. Every step that made no sense. He has been there. No matter how hard the journey has been, the Father has always been carrying us.

And he has always been carrying you.

So don't quit in the desert. Don't decide to go back to Egypt. Even if you're afraid, don't get out now. When you know how the story ends, you don't have to be worried about a bad chapter—or a few bad ones in a row.

Just because my daughter has *yet* to be healed doesn't mean she won't be. And just because your breakthrough hasn't come *yet* doesn't mean it won't. So don't put a period where God has a comma. Don't say "The End" while God is still writing.

A great cloud follower once said, "Even though I walk through the valley of the shadow of death, I will fear no evil, for you are with me" (Psalm 23:4). The Good Shepherd leads you through the valley you don't want to go through to get you to green pastures you need.

> The Good Shepherd leads you through the valley you don't want to go through to get you to green pastures you need.

And only those who follow him all the way through the valley of the shadow of death *know* that the Shepherd is good. Until then, it's just theory.

I share this with you because I'm in the middle of this journey too. I don't have it all figured out. I don't understand it all. I haven't arrived. But I wholeheartedly believe that the pathway to a life of freedom is to follow the cloud one next step at a time.

So I follow.

Even when it's hard. Even when the valley is so dark that I can see only the step right in front of me.

And I hope you will too.

I follow because I believe that with every step, he isn't just leading me but *carrying* me to green pastures and quiet waters. With every step, he restores my soul.

You might be wondering . . .

How should I deal with this difficulty? Follow the cloud.

How should I make this decision? Follow the cloud.

What should I do in the midst of my pain? Follow the cloud.

Where should I go next? Follow the cloud.

What's God's plan for my life? Follow the cloud.

Follow the cloud because he is faithful to the end. He has carried you out of Egypt, across the sea, through the desert, and beyond the wilderness, graciously moving one step at a time toward the Promised Land. And every time you look back, you'll see his faithfulness. The psalmist who walked through the valley looked back on his journey and declared, "Surely goodness and mercy shall follow me all the days of my life" (Psalm 23:6, NKJV). He discovered that while he was following the cloud, goodness and mercy were following him.

No matter where the cloud leads you, the Good Shepherd is always in front of you, and goodness and mercy are always behind you. Therefore, where the cloud is going is the safest place to be, especially when the valley is dark.

KIDS' THEOLOGY

Every night when I tuck my kids into bed, I tell them who they are.

"Trey, you are like King David. You have a warrior spirit and a tender heart."

"Emma, you are a bold leader with a heart of worship."

And then I ask them, "What do you need to always remember?"

They say the same four things every night. "God is good. Jesus has forgiven me. I am loved. And everything is possible." That's foundational theology that most adults don't believe. It's the kid's version of the three circles. The desire of the *Father's heart (God is good)* is that we would *receive his grace (Jesus has forgiven me), experience his presence (I am loved),* and *release his kingdom (Everything is possible).*

Every step we refuse to take can be traced back to our doubt in one of those areas. When we don't believe that God is good, Jesus has forgiven us, we are loved, and that everything is possible, we won't follow the cloud; we will follow ourselves. But what if we did believe it?

What if *you* believe it?

What if you believed that because God is good, he sent Jesus to fully forgive you? What if you believed that because you are forgiven, you can rest in the fullness of his love? What if you believed that because you are loved, everything is now possible? How different would your life be? That is the journey the cloud is leading you on: not only to discover but also experience this truth. With each step you take, you discover who you are, who he is, and what you were created to do. The fullness of the kingdom belongs to those who live in the Father's heart with child-like faith.

In Jesus, you have been set free. But there is a big difference between being set free and living free. Just because you have received the gift of salvation doesn't mean you're living in the fullness of the freedom he offers.

Simply ask the Israelites.

Freedom is not a onetime event; it's a lifestyle. And it's only in following the cloud that we learn to live free. Like it was for the Israelites, every step God asks you to take is an invitation to press on toward freedom or go back to bondage.

So here's the question: What is the Holy Spirit saying to you, and what is your next step? What has he been whispering to you, and what are you going to do with what you have heard?

Your Promised Land is waiting. The Father's love is calling you home. God is good. Jesus has forgiven you. You are loved. And everything is possible. So what are you waiting for? Ask. Listen. Respond.

Follow the cloud. Live free.

Follow the Cloud—Live Free

God is good.
Jesus has forgiven me.
I am loved.
Everything is possible.

Which of those do you struggle to believe the most? Why?

The cloud is on the move, and it is time to respond.

My very next step is_____
_____.

I am going to share this step with _____
and ask him/her to hold me accountable to take it.

ACKNOWLEDGMENTS

No one follows the cloud alone. Our next steps are intimately connected to those around us.

Colleen, every day you inspire me with your faith, hope, and love. I have watched you say "Yes" to God even when it cost you everything. Thank you for serving Emma in a way no one but me ever sees—you follow the cloud when most would have gone back home. I love you.

Trey and Emma Joy, thank you for teaching me more about God than I have been able to teach you. I can't wait to see where the cloud leads you.

Mom, you are my biggest encourager. Thanks for always believing in me. Your endless prayers are the very fiber and fabric of this book. Dad, thanks for living the kind of life I want to live. You have always been my role model and not too many guys get to say that.

Mom and Dad Evans, thank you for entrusting me with Colleen and for being a picture of people who always follow God.

Valley Creek Elders (Brad Lanham, Don Manning, Ken Lancaster, Robert Maxey, Justin Nall, and Ben Moreno), thank you for taking a chance on a twenty-nine-year-old kid. You live this message of hearing God's voice and following by faith even when it seems crazy to everyone else.

To the original leadership team (Ben Moreno, Becca Reynolds, Josh Wintermute, Dawn Shapley, and Chris Pitt), who would of thought, huh? I don't think any of us would have guessed that all those countless meetings in room 207 would have turned into what Valley Creek is today. Thank you for believing in the dream. I guess big things really do start small.

To our now much bigger team, thank you for following Jesus so well. Like we always say, "We want to do this a long time together." Thank you for finding *your* voice in *our* dream.

Kevin and Lisa Evans, thank you for taking your next step so I could take mine. Steve Dulin and Joe Martin, thank you for overseeing us with grace and truth. John Blase, Pam Shoup, and the entire team at WaterBrook Multnomah, thank you for taking a chance on this first time author. Thank you for giving this message a voice. Justin Nall, thank you for being a great friend. Ben Moreno, thanks for pulling the rocks out of my heart. Becca Reynolds, thank you for always making things "great."

Josh Wintermute, thanks for bringing so much laughter into my life. Cherie Hoover, thank you for helping me in more ways than you know.

Finally, Valley Creekers, thank you for a being a church who asks, listens, and responds to God. You are easy to lead because you are quick to follow Jesus. May we never take for granted what a privilege it is to be a part of what God is doing among us. The best is yet to come because the cloud is on the move!